2023 Latest
Instant Pot Cookbook

1800+	Super-Easy & Healthy Instant Pot Recipes Perfect for Your Super Shortcut Instant Pot, Step By Step for Home cooking

Maria F. Coyle

CONTENTS

INTRODUCTION 7

CHAPTER 1 BASIC INFORMATION OF 1800 RECIPES INSTANT POT
COOKBOOK 8

Why Instant Pot Cooking Is Healthier? 8
General Precautions To Keep in Mind 8

MEASUREMENT CONVERSIONS 9

CHAPTER 2 BREAKFAST 11

Hard-"boiled" Eggs 12
Bacon Cheddar Scrambled Egg Muffins 12
Crustless Crab Quiche 12
Bacon-poblano Morning Taters 13
Sweet Potato Morning Hash 13
Western Omelet Casserole 13
Honey Butternut Squash Cake Oatmeal 13
Cinnamon Roll Doughnut Holes 14
Egg Muffins To Go 14
California Frittata Bake 14
Pumpkin Steel Cut Oats With Cinnamon 15
Sunday Brunch Sausage Gravy 15
Crustless Power Quiche 15
Breakfast Frittata 15
Georgia Peach French Toast Casserole 16
Pumpkin Muffins 16
Banana & Vanilla Pancakes 16
Spinach & Feta Pie With Cherry Tomatoes 17
French Cheese & Spinach Quiche 17
Tofu Hash Brown Breakfast 17
Light & Fruity Yogurt 17
Strawberry Jam 18
Greek Yogurt With Honey & Walnuts 18
Chicken Sandwiches With Barbecue Sauce 18
Buckwheat Pancake With Yogurt & Berries 18
Lazy Steel Cut Oats With Coconut 19
Smoked Salmon & Egg Muffins 19
Lemony Pancake Bites With Blueberry Syrup 19

CHAPTER 3 APPETIZERS, SOUPS & SIDES.................20

Chorizo Soup With Roasted Tomatoes 21
Broccoli-gruyère Soup 21
Garbanzo Stew With Onions & Tomatoes 22
Savory Butternut Squash Soup 22
Frittata With Vegetables & Cheese 22
Mushroom-potato Hash Casserole 22
Classic Palak Paneer Dip 23
Kimchi Ramen Noodle Soup 23
Dilled Salmon Soup 23
Gingered Sweet Potatoes 23
Simple Onion Cheese Soup 24
Aromatic Lamb Stew 24
Pea & Garbanzo Bean Soup 24
Wild Mushroom Soup 24
Creamy Chicken Soup 25
Milk-boiled Corn On The Cob 25
Broccoli & Mushroom Egg Cups 25
Potatoes & Tuna Salad With Pickles 25
Moroccan Lentil Soup 26
Chowder With Broccoli, Carrot & Tofu 26
Loaded Broccoli 26
Rosemary Potato Fries 26
Lentil Pâté 27
Quick Chicken Soup 27
Simple Carrot & Oregano Soup 27
Broccoli & Egg Salad 27
Pizza-style Stuffed Mushrooms 28
Rustic Soup With Turkey Balls & Carrots 28

CHAPTER 4 POULTRY 29

Creamy Pesto Chicken 30
Spring Onion Buffalo Wings 30
Chicken & Zucchini Pilaf 30
Saucy Chicken Marsala 31
Hot Chicken With Coriander & Ginger 31
Korean-style Chicken 31
Hot Chicken With Garlic & Mushrooms 31
Rigatoni With Turkey & Tomato Sauce 32
Chicken Gumbo 32
Curried Chicken With Mushrooms 32
Jamaican Chicken With Pineapple Sauce 32
Turkey & Black Bean Chili 33
Caribbean Turkey Wings 33
Bell Pepper & Chicken Stew 33
Weekend Turkey With Vegetables 33
Quinoa Pilaf With Chicken 34

Macaroni With Chicken & Pesto Sauce 34
Garlic Chicken 34
Easy Chicken With Capers & Tomatoes 34
Sweet & Citrusy Chicken Breasts 35
Honey-glazed Turkey 35
Turkey Cakes With Ginger Gravy 35
Spicy Honey Chicken 36
Sticky Chicken Wings 36
Chimichurri Chicken 36
Best Italian Chicken Balls 36
Awesome Chicken In Tikka Masala Sauce 37
Turkey Stew With Salsa Verde 37

CHAPTER 5 PORK, BEEF & LAMB 38

Classic Beef Stroganoff 39
Easy Wax Beans With Ground Beef 39
Pork Chops With Creamy Gravy & Broccoli 39
Short Ribs With Wine Mushroom Sauce 40
Delicious Pork In Button Mushroom Gravy 40
Lamb Chorba 40
Beef Tikka Masala 41
Best Pork Chops With Bbq Sauce & Veggies 41
Melt-in-your-mouth Meatballs 41
Traditional Lamb With Vegetables 41
Easy Pork Fillets With Peachy Sauce 42
Pulled Pork 42
Leftover Beef Sandwiches 42
Maple Pork Carnitas 43
Quick French-style Lamb With Sesame 43
Cilantro Pork With Avocado 43
Pear & Cider Pork Tenderloin 43
Pork With Onions & Cream Sauce 44
Tasty Beef Cutlets With Vegetables 44
Gruyere Mushroom & Mortadella Cups 44
Quick And Easy Meatloaf 44
Bbq Pork Lettuce Cups 45
Easy Lamb & Spinach Soup 45
Wine Pork Butt With Fennel & Mushrooms 45
Hot Paprika & Oregano Lamb 45
Chipotle Shredded Beef 46
Beef Meatballs With Tomato-basil Sauce 46
Beef Neapolitan Ragù 46

CHAPTER 6 FISH & SEAFOOD 47

Seafood Chowder With Oyster Crackers 48
Stuffed Tench With Herbs & Lemon 48
Dilled Salmon Fillets 48
Tangy Shrimp Curry 49
Lobster Risotto 49
Mediterranean Cod With Cherry Tomatoes 49
Seafood Medley With Rosemary Rice 50
Spicy Haddock With Beer & Potatoes 50
Herby Crab Legs With Lemon 50
Octopus & Shrimp With Collard Greens 50
Creamy Wild Salmon 51
Paprika Salmon With Dill Sauce 51
Chili Squid 51
Pistachio-crusted Halibut 51
Shrimp Boil With Chorizo Sausages 52
Haddock With Edamame Soybeans 52
Herby Trout With Farro & Green Beans 52
Beer-steamed Shrimp 52
Cheesy Tuna 53
Mint Salmon On Spinach Bed 53
Shrimp Fajitas 53
Basil Clams With Garlic & White Wine 53
Cheesy Shrimp Scampi 54
White Wine Marinated Squid Rings 54
Louisiana Grouper 54
Spicy Salmon With Oregano & Sea Salt 55
Creole Shrimp With Okra 55
Mediterranean Cod With Capers 55

CHAPTER 7 VEGAN & VEGETARIAN 56

Sautéed Spinach With Roquefort Cheese 57
Quick Cassoulet 57
Millet Eggplant Pilaf 57
Power Green Soup With Lasagna Noodles 58
Spicy Split Pea Stew 58
Curly Kale Soup 58
Easy Tahini Sweet Potato Mash 58
Parmesan Topped Vegetable Mash 59
White Bean Cassoulet 59
Zucchini Pomodoro 59
Hot Tofu Meatballs 60
Steamed Artichokes With Lime Aioli 60
Sweet Polenta With Pistachios 60
Speedy Mac & Goat Cheese 60
Stuffed Potatoes With Feta & Rosemary 61
Homemade Gazpacho Soup 61

Celery & Red Bean Stew 61
Coconut Millet Porridge 61
Coconut Milk Millet Pudding 62
Cali Dogs 62
Easy Cheesy Mac 62
Gingery Butternut Squash Soup..62
Turmeric Stew With Green Peas 63
Savory Spinach With Mashed Potatoes 63
Vegetarian Green Dip..63
Bavarian Kale And Potatoes 63
Wheat Berry Salad 64
Steamed Artichokes & Green Beans..64

CHAPTER 8 BEANS, RICE, & GRAINS 65

Boston Baked Beans 66
Green Goddess Mac 'n' Cheese 66
Wild Rice Pilaf..66
Vegetable Paella 67
Quinoa Bowls With Broccoli & Pesto 67
Spicy Three-bean Vegetable Chili 67
Ham & Peas With Goat Cheese 67
Cheesy Mushrooms With Garganelli 68
Lentil-spinach Curry 68
Down South Savory Porridge 68
Beef Pasta Alla Parmigiana..68
Cajun Red Beans 69
Date & Apple Risotto 69
Red Beans And Chorizo 69
Jamaican Cornmeal Porridge 70
Easy Red Lentil Dhal With Spinach 70
Pancetta With Garbanzo Beans 70
Couscous With Lamb & Vegetables..70
Coconut Rice Breakfast 71
Pomegranate Rice With Vegetables 71
Cheesy Polenta With Sundried Tomatoes 71
Tomato & Mushroom Rotini 71
Spinach-feta Risotto..72
Easy Brown Rice With Sunflower Seeds 72
Risotto With Broccoli & Grana Padano 72
Greek-style Navy Beans 72
Tomato & Feta Pearl Barley 73
Mexican Pinto Beans 73

CHAPTER 9 DESSERTS & DRINKS 74

Carrot Coconut Cake..75
Cinnamon Applesauce 75
Stuffed Apples..75
Amazing Fruity Cheesecake 76
Hot Cocoa Brownies 76
Cottage Cheesecake With Strawberries 76
Chocolate Glazed Cake...77
Banana Bread Pudding..77
Banana & Walnut Oatmeal 77
Pie Cups With Fruit Filling 77
Simple Apple Cinnamon Dessert..78
Root Beer Float Cupcakes 78
Easy Lemon Cake 78
Spiced Peaches With Cinnamon Whipped Cream 79
Lemon-apricot Compote 79
Grandma's Fruit Compote...79
Vanilla Cheesecake With Cranberry Filling 79
Spiced & Warming Mulled Wine 80
Chocolate Custard...80
Rice Pudding...80
Orange New York Cheesecake 81
Steamed Bread Pudding..81
Cinnamon Brown Rice Pudding 81
Homemade Spanish-style Horchata 82
Plum & Almond Dessert 82
Walnut & Pumpkin Tart 82
Molten Chocolate Cake...83
Yogurt Cheesecake With Cranberries 83

APPENDIX : RECIPES INDEX 84

INTRODUCTION

Hi, I'm Maria, the author of this latest Instant Pot recipe book for 2023. I am a former physician's assistant with a busy schedule and the need to take care of my 3 children. As busy as I was, I didn't want to sacrifice my kids' healthy diet, which I think all parents want, so I wrote this series of healthy recipes for instant pot.

Welcome to the ultimate collection of Instant Pot recipes that will revolutionize your kitchen! With over 1800 delicious recipes, this cookbook is the perfect guide to help you create mouthwatering dishes in the Instant Pot.

Whether you're a busy parent looking to save time on meal prep, a home cook searching for new and exciting recipes to try, or someone who just wants to eat healthier and more flavorful meals, this cookbook has something for everyone.

Inside, you'll find a vast selection of recipes ranging from breakfast, lunch, and dinner to appetizers, snacks, and desserts. All of the recipes are carefully crafted to be easy to follow and use simple ingredients that are readily available in your local grocery store.

With this cookbook, you'll discover the full potential of the Instant Pot and its many features, including pressure cooking, slow cooking, sautéing, and more. Plus, you'll learn valuable tips and tricks that will help you get the most out of your Instant Pot and achieve perfect results every time.

So, whether you're a seasoned Instant Pot pro or just starting your journey, this cookbook will be your go-to guide for creating delicious and healthy meals for your family and friends. Get ready to experience the ultimate in convenience, flavor, and nutrition with the 1800 Days Recipes Instant Pot Cookbook!

Why Instant Pot Cooking Is Healthier?

There's no denying that an Instant Pot® is a must-have for every kitchen. What's not to love about a slow-cooker, pressure cooker and stovetop stand-in all wrapped into one compact appliance? With a few accessories and the right recipes, your multicooker can get cozy soups, crowd-pleasing chicken dinners, healthy weeknight meals and even desserts on the table with ease. Ready to put your Instant Pot® to good use? You're in the right place — we've got plenty of delicious options for you to choose from.

Instant Pot cooking can be considered healthier for several reasons. Firstly, it reduces cooking time, which means that food retains more of its nutrients, flavors, and textures. Secondly, the Instant Pot requires less oil and fat to cook food compared to traditional cooking methods, making it a healthier option for those who are conscious about their fat intake.

Additionally, the Instant Pot is designed to retain moisture and prevent evaporation, which can help to preserve the natural flavors and juices of the food. And Instant Pot cooking can retain more nutrients than other methods because the cooking time is shorter, which means the food is exposed to heat for a shorter period. Finally, the Instant Pot allows for cooking with wholesome ingredients like whole grains, beans, and vegetables, making it a healthier option overall.

General Precautions To Keep in Mind

Read the manual: Make sure to read the Instant Pot manual thoroughly before using it for the first time. This will help you understand the features and functions of the appliance and ensure you use it safely.

Use enough liquid: The Instant Pot requires liquid to create steam and build pressure, which is necessary for cooking food. Make sure to use the recommended amount of liquid for each recipe, and never fill the pot more than 2/3 full.

Don't overfill: It's important not to overfill the Instant Pot, as this can cause food to get stuck to the lid or result in uneven cooking. Stick to the recommended capacity for your specific model.

Use caution when releasing pressure: The Instant Pot can release steam and hot liquid quickly, so use caution when releasing pressure. Always follow the instructions for releasing pressure, and avoid putting your face or hands directly over the valve.

Keep the lid and sealing ring clean: Make sure to keep the Instant Pot lid and sealing ring clean and free from debris. This will ensure that the pot seals properly and maintains pressure while cooking.

Use caution when cooking with oil: If you're using oil in your Instant Pot, be sure to use caution when adding it to the pot. The oil can heat up quickly and cause hot splatters, so pour it in slowly and carefully.

By following these precautions, you can use your Instant Pot safely and enjoy delicious meals cooked quickly and easily.

Measurement Conversions

BASIC KITCHEN CONVERSIONS & EQUIVALENTS

DRY MEASUREMENTS CONVERSION CHART

3 TEASPOONS = 1 TABLESPOON = 1/16 CUP

6 TEASPOONS = 2 TABLESPOONS = 1/8 CUP

12 TEASPOONS = 4 TABLESPOONS = 1/4 CUP

24 TEASPOONS = 8 TABLESPOONS = 1/2 CUP

36 TEASPOONS = 12 TABLESPOONS = 3/4 CUP

48 TEASPOONS = 16 TABLESPOONS = 1 CUP

METRIC TO US COOKING CONVERSIONS

OVEN TEMPERATURES

120 °C = 250 °F

160 °C = 320 °F

180° C = 350 °F

205 °C = 400 °F

220 °C = 425 °F

LIQUID MEASUREMENTS CONVERSION CHART

8 FLUID OUNCES = 1 CUP = 1/2 PINT = 1/4 QUART

16 FLUID OUNCES = 2 CUPS = 1 PINT = 1/2 QUART

32 FLUID OUNCES = 4 CUPS = 2 PINTS = 1 QUART
  = 1/4 GALLON

128 FLUID OUNCES = 16 CUPS = 8 PINTS = 4 QUARTS = 1 GALLON

BAKING IN GRAMS

1 CUP FLOUR = 140 GRAMS

1 CUP SUGAR = 150 GRAMS

1 CUP POWDERED SUGAR = 160 GRAMS

1 CUP HEAVY CREAM = 235 GRAMS

VOLUME

1 MILLILITER = 1/5 TEASPOON

5 ML = 1 TEASPOON

15 ML = 1 TABLESPOON

240 ML = 1 CUP OR 8 FLUID OUNCES

1 LITER = 34 FL. OUNCES

WEIGHT

1 GRAM = .035 OUNCES

100 GRAMS = 3.5 OUNCES

500 GRAMS = 1.1 POUNDS

1 KILOGRAM = 35 OUNCES

US TO METRIC COOKING CONVERSIONS

1/5 TSP = 1 ML

1 TSP = 5 ML

1 TBSP = 15 ML

1 FL OUNCE = 30 ML

1 CUP = 237 ML

1 PINT (2 CUPS) = 473 ML

1 QUART (4 CUPS) = .95 LITER

1 GALLON (16 CUPS) = 3.8 LITERS

1 OZ = 28 GRAMS

1 POUND = 454 GRAMS

BUTTER

1 CUP BUTTER = 2 STICKS = 8 OUNCES = 230 GRAMS = 8 TABLESPOONS

WHAT DOES 1 CUP EQUAL

1 CUP = 8 FLUID OUNCES

1 CUP = 16 TABLESPOONS

1 CUP = 48 TEASPOONS

1 CUP = 1/2 PINT

1 CUP = 1/4 QUART

1 CUP = 1/16 GALLON

1 CUP = 240 ML

BAKING PAN CONVERSIONS

1 CUP ALL-PURPOSE FLOUR = 4.5 OZ

1 CUP ROLLED OATS = 3 OZ 1 LARGE EGG = 1.7 OZ

1 CUP BUTTER = 8 OZ 1 CUP MILK = 8 OZ

1 CUP HEAVY CREAM = 8.4 OZ

1 CUP GRANULATED SUGAR = 7.1 OZ

1 CUP PACKED BROWN SUGAR = 7.75 OZ

1 CUP VEGETABLE OIL = 7.7 OZ

1 CUP UNSIFTED POWDERED SUGAR = 4.4 OZ

BAKING PAN CONVERSIONS

9-INCH ROUND CAKE PAN = 12 CUPS

10-INCH TUBE PAN =16 CUPS

11-INCH BUNDT PAN = 12 CUPS

9-INCH SPRINGFORM PAN = 10 CUPS

9 X 5 INCH LOAF PAN = 8 CUPS

9-INCH SQUARE PAN = 8 CUPS

Chapter 2 Breakfast

Chapter 2 Breakfast

Hard-"boiled" Eggs

Servings:6
Cooking Time: 6 Minutes

Ingredients:
- 1 cup water
- 6 large eggs

Directions:
1. Add water to the Instant Pot and insert steamer basket. Place eggs in basket. Lock lid.
2. Press the Manual or Pressure Cook button and adjust time to 6 minutes. When timer beeps, quick-release pressure until float valve drops. Unlock lid.
3. Create an ice bath by adding 1 cup ice and 1 cup water to a medium bowl. Transfer eggs to ice bath to stop the cooking process.
4. Peel eggs. Slice each egg directly onto a plate. Serve immediately.

Bacon Cheddar Scrambled Egg Muffins

Servings:6
Cooking Time: 8 Minutes

Ingredients:
- 4 large eggs
- 2 tablespoons whole milk
- 2 tablespoons grated yellow onion
- ½ teaspoon salt
- ½ teaspoon ground black pepper
- 5 slices bacon, cooked and crumbled
- ¼ cup grated Cheddar cheese
- 1 cup water

Directions:
1. Grease six silicone cupcake liners.
2. In a medium bowl, whisk together eggs, milk, onion, salt, and pepper. Distribute egg mixture evenly among cupcake liners. Add equal amounts of bacon and cheese to each cup.
3. Add water to the Instant Pot and insert steam rack. Place steamer basket on steam rack. Carefully place muffin cups in basket. Lock lid.
4. Press the Manual or Pressure Cook button and adjust time to 8 minutes. When timer beeps, quick-release pressure until float valve drops. Unlock lid.
5. Remove egg muffins. Serve warm.

Crustless Crab Quiche

Servings:6
Cooking Time: 10 Minutes

Ingredients:
- 6 large eggs
- ¼ cup unsweetened almond milk
- 2 teaspoons fresh thyme leaves
- ½ teaspoon sea salt
- ¼ teaspoon ground black pepper
- ½ teaspoon hot sauce
- ½ pound crabmeat
- ¼ cup crumbled goat cheese
- 2 thick slices bacon, diced
- ¼ cup peeled and diced onion
- ¼ cup seeded and diced green bell pepper
- 2 cups water

Directions:
1. In a medium bowl, whisk eggs, milk, thyme leaves, salt, pepper, and hot sauce. Stir in crabmeat and goat cheese. Set aside.
2. Grease a 7-cup glass dish. Set aside.
3. Press the Sauté button on Instant Pot. Add diced bacon and brown for 2 minutes, rendering some fat. Add onion and bell pepper and stir-fry with bacon until tender. Transfer mixture to the glass container. Pour in egg mixture.
4. Place trivet in Instant Pot. Pour in water. Place dish with egg mixture onto trivet. Lock lid.
5. Press the Manual button and adjust time to 5 minutes. When timer beeps, let pressure release naturally for 10 minutes. Quick-release any additional pressure until float valve drops and then unlock lid.
6. Remove dish from Instant Pot. Let cool for 10 minutes to allow eggs to set. Slice and serve.

Bacon-poblano Morning Taters

Servings:4
Cooking Time: 10 Minutes

Ingredients:
- 1 tablespoon olive oil
- 2 slices bacon, diced
- 1 small onion, peeled and diced
- 2 small poblano peppers, seeded and diced
- 4 cups small-diced russet potatoes
- 2 tablespoons ghee
- 2–3 cloves garlic, minced
- 1 teaspoon sea salt
- ½ teaspoon ground black pepper
- ½ cup water

Directions:
1. Press Sauté button on Instant Pot and heat oil. Add bacon, onion, and peppers. Stir-fry until onions are translucent, 3–5 minutes. Transfer mixture to a 7-cup glass dish. Toss in potatoes, ghee, garlic, salt, and pepper.
2. Insert trivet into Instant Pot. Pour in water. Place dish on trivet. Lock lid.
3. Press the Manual button and adjust time to 5 minutes. When the timer beeps, let the pressure release naturally until the float valve drops. Remove dish from pot and serve.

Sweet Potato Morning Hash

Servings:4
Cooking Time: 10 Minutes

Ingredients:
- 6 large eggs
- 1 tablespoon Italian seasoning
- ½ teaspoon sea salt
- ½ teaspoon ground black pepper
- ½ pound ground pork sausage
- 1 large sweet potato, peeled and cubed
- 1 small onion, peeled and diced
- 2 cloves garlic, minced
- 1 medium green bell pepper, seeded and diced
- 2 cups water

Directions:
1. In a medium bowl, whisk together eggs, Italian seasoning, salt, and pepper. Set aside.
2. Press the Sauté button on Instant Pot. Stir-fry sausage, sweet potato, onion, garlic, and bell pepper for 3–5 minutes until onions are translucent.
3. Transfer mixture to a 7-cup greased glass dish. Pour whisked eggs over the sausage mixture.
4. Place trivet in Instant Pot. Pour in water. Place dish with egg mixture onto trivet. Lock lid.
5. Press the Manual button and adjust time to 5 minutes. When timer beeps, quick-release pressure until float valve drops and then unlock lid. Remove dish from Instant Pot. Let sit at room temperature for 5–10 minutes to allow the eggs to set. Slice and serve.

Western Omelet Casserole

Servings:4
Cooking Time: 10 Minutes

Ingredients:
- 6 large eggs
- ½ teaspoon sea salt
- ½ teaspoon ground black pepper
- 2 dashes hot sauce
- 1 cup diced ham
- 1 small red bell pepper, seeded and diced
- 1 small green bell pepper, seeded and diced
- 1 small onion, peeled and diced
- 2 cups water

Directions:
1. In a medium bowl, whisk together eggs, salt, pepper, and hot sauce. Set aside.
2. Press the Sauté button on Instant Pot. Stir-fry ham, bell peppers, and onion for 3–5 minutes or until onions are translucent.
3. Transfer mixture to a greased 7-cup glass dish. Pour whisked eggs over the ham mixture.
4. Place trivet in Instant Pot. Pour in water. Place dish with egg mixture onto trivet. Lock lid.
5. Press the Manual button and adjust time to 5 minutes. When timer beeps, quick-release pressure until float valve drops and then unlock lid.
6. Remove dish from the Instant Pot. Let sit at room temperature for 5–10 minutes to allow the eggs to set. Slice and serve.

Honey Butternut Squash Cake Oatmeal

Servings: 4
Cooking Time: 35 Minutes

Ingredients:
- 3 ½ cups coconut milk
- 1 cup steel-cut oats
- 8 oz butternut squash, grated
- ½ cup sultanas
- 1/3 cup honey

- ¾ tsp ground ginger
- ½ tsp salt
- ½ tsp orange zest
- ¼ tsp ground nutmeg
- ¼ cup walnuts, chopped
- ½ tsp vanilla extract
- ½ tsp sugar

Directions:

1. In the cooker, mix sultanas, orange zest, ginger, milk, honey, butternut squash, salt, oats, and nutmeg. Seal the lid and cook on High Pressure for 12 minutes. Do a natural release for 10 minutes. Into the oatmeal, stir in the vanilla extract and sugar. Top with walnuts and serve.

Cinnamon Roll Doughnut Holes

Servings:14
Cooking Time: 16 Minutes

Ingredients:

- 1 package Krusteaz Cinnamon Roll Supreme Mix (includes icing packet)
- 6 tablespoons unsalted butter, melted
- ½ cup cold water
- ¼ cup chopped pecans
- 1 cup water

Directions:

1. In a medium bowl, combine dry mix, butter, and ½ cup cold water. Fold in pecans. Spoon half of batter into a greased seven-hole silicone egg mold. If your egg mold has a silicone top, use this. If your egg mold came with a plastic top, do not use. Instead, cover with aluminum foil.
2. Add 1 cup water to the Instant Pot and insert steam rack. Place egg mold on steam rack. Lock lid.
3. Press the Manual or Pressure Cook button and adjust time to 8 minutes. When timer beeps, quick-release pressure until float valve drops. Unlock lid.
4. Pop doughnut holes out of egg mold and repeat with remaining batter.
5. When doughnut holes are cooled, mix icing packet with 1 ½ tablespoons water and dip doughnut holes into glaze to cover. Serve.

Egg Muffins To Go

Servings:3
Cooking Time: 15 Minutes

Ingredients:

- 1 tablespoon olive oil
- 3 pieces bacon, diced
- 1 small onion, peeled and diced

- 4 large eggs
- 2 teaspoons Italian seasoning
- ½ teaspoon sea salt
- ½ teaspoon ground black pepper
- ¼ cup shredded Cheddar cheese
- 1 small Roma tomato, diced
- ¼ cup chopped spinach
- 1 cup water

Directions:

1. Press the Sauté button on Instant Pot. Heat olive oil. Add bacon and onion and stir-fry 3–5 minutes until onions are translucent. Transfer mixture to a small bowl to cool.
2. In a medium bowl, whisk together eggs, Italian seasoning, salt, black pepper, cheese, tomatoes, and spinach. Stir in cooled bacon mixture.
3. Place trivet into Instant Pot. Pour in water. Place steamer basket on trivet.
4. Distribute egg mixture evenly among 6 silicone muffin cups. Carefully place cups on steamer basket. Lock lid.
5. Press the Manual button and adjust time to 8 minutes. When the timer beeps, quick-release pressure until float valve drops and then unlock lid.
6. Remove egg muffins and serve warm.

California Frittata Bake

Servings:4
Cooking Time: 10 Minutes

Ingredients:

- 4 large eggs
- 4 large egg whites
- ½ teaspoon sea salt
- ¼ teaspoon ground black pepper
- ¼ cup chopped fresh basil
- ½ cup chopped spinach
- 2 small Roma tomatoes, diced
- 1 medium avocado, pitted and diced
- ¼ cup grated Gruyère cheese
- 1 tablespoon avocado oil
- 1 pound ground chicken
- 1 small onion, peeled and diced
- 1 cup water

Directions:

1. In a medium bowl, whisk together eggs, egg whites, salt, and pepper. Add basil, spinach, tomatoes, avocado, and cheese. Set aside.
2. Press the Sauté button on Instant Pot. Heat the avocado oil and stir-fry chicken and onion for approximately 5 minutes or until chicken is no longer pink.
3. Transfer cooked mixture to a 7-cup greased glass dish and set aside to cool. Once cool pour whisked eggs over the

chicken mixture and stir to combine.

4. Place trivet in Instant Pot. Pour in water. Place dish with egg mixture onto trivet. Lock lid.

5. Press the Manual button and adjust time to 5 minutes. When the timer beeps, let pressure release naturally until the float valve drops and then unlock the lid.

6. Remove dish from the Instant Pot and set aside for 5–10 minutes to allow the eggs to set. Slice and serve.

Pumpkin Steel Cut Oats With Cinnamon

Servings: 4
Cooking Time: 25 Minutes

Ingredients:
- 1 tbsp butter
- 2 cups steel-cut oats
- ¼ tsp cinnamon
- 1 cup pumpkin puree
- 3 tbsp maple syrup
- 2 tsp pumpkin seeds, toasted

Directions:
1. Melt butter on Sauté. Add in cinnamon, oats, pumpkin puree, and 3 cups of water. Seal the lid, select Porridge and cook for 10 minutes on High Pressure to get a few bite oats or for 14 minutes to form soft oats. Do a quick release. Open the lid and stir in maple syrup. Top with pumpkin seeds and serve.

Sunday Brunch Sausage Gravy

Servings:10
Cooking Time: 10 Minutes

Ingredients:
- 2 tablespoons butter
- 1 pound ground pork sausage
- 1 small sweet onion, peeled and diced
- ¼ cup chicken broth
- ¼ cup all-purpose flour
- 1½ cups heavy cream
- ½ teaspoon sea salt
- 1 tablespoon ground black pepper

Directions:
1. Press the Sauté button on the Instant Pot. Add butter and heat until melted. Add pork sausage and onion. Stir-fry 3–5 minutes until onions are translucent. The pork will still be a little pink in places. Add chicken broth. Lock lid.

2. Press the Manual button and adjust time to 1 minute. When the timer beeps, quick-release the pressure until the float valve drops and then unlock the lid. Whisk in flour, cream, salt, and pepper.

3. Press the Keep Warm button and let the gravy sit for about 5–10 minutes to allow the sauce to thicken. Remove from heat and serve warm.

Crustless Power Quiche

Servings:2
Cooking Time: 9 Minutes

Ingredients:
- 6 large eggs
- ½ teaspoon salt
- ½ teaspoon ground black pepper
- 2 teaspoons olive oil
- ½ cup diced red onion
- 1 medium red bell pepper, seeded and diced
- ¼ pound ground pork sausage
- 1 ½ cups water
- 1 medium avocado, peeled, pitted, and diced

Directions:
1. In a medium bowl, whisk together eggs, salt, and black pepper. Set aside.

2. Press the Sauté button on the Instant Pot and heat oil. Stir-fry onion, bell pepper, and sausage 3–4 minutes until sausage starts to brown and onions are tender. Press the Cancel button.

3. Transfer sausage mixture to a greased 7-cup glass bowl. Pour whisked eggs over the mixture.

4. Add water to the Instant Pot and insert steam rack. Place bowl with egg mixture on steam rack. Lock lid.

5. Press the Manual or Pressure Cook button and adjust time to 5 minutes. When timer beeps, quick-release pressure until float valve drops. Unlock lid.

6. Remove bowl from pot. Let sit at room temperature 5–10 minutes to allow the eggs to set, then remove quiche from bowl, slice, and garnish with avocado. Serve warm.

Breakfast Frittata

Servings: 4
Cooking Time: 25 Minutes

Ingredients:
- 8 beaten eggs
- 1 cup cherry tomatoes, halved
- 1 tbsp Dijon mustard
- 1 cup mushrooms, chopped
- Salt and pepper to taste
- 1 cup sharp cheddar, grated

Directions:

1. Combine the eggs, mushrooms, mustard, salt, pepper, and ½ cup of cheddar cheese in a bowl. Pour in a greased baking pan and top with the remaining cheddar cheese and cherry tomatoes. Add 1 cup of water to your Instant Pot and fit in a trivet. Place the baking pan on the trivet.

2. Seal the lid. Select Manual and cook for 15 minutes on High. When ready, perform a quick pressure release and unlock the lid. Slice into wedges before serving.

Georgia Peach French Toast Casserole

Servings:4
Cooking Time: 20 Minutes

Ingredients:
- 4 cups cubed French bread, dried out overnight
- 2 cups diced, peeled ripe peaches
- 1 cup whole milk
- 3 large eggs
- 1 teaspoon vanilla extract
- ¼ cup granulated sugar
- ⅛ teaspoon salt
- 3 tablespoons unsalted butter, cut into 3 pats
- 1 cup water

Directions:
1. Grease a 7-cup glass baking dish. Add bread to dish in an even layer. Add peaches in an even layer over bread. Set aside.

2. In a medium bowl, whisk together milk, eggs, vanilla, sugar, and salt. Pour over bread; place butter pats on top.

3. Add water to the Instant Pot and insert steam rack. Place glass baking dish on top of steam rack. Lock lid.

4. Press the Manual or Pressure Cook button and adjust time to 20 minutes. When timer beeps, quick-release pressure until float valve drops. Unlock lid.

5. Remove bowl and transfer to a cooling rack until set, about 20 minutes. Serve.

Pumpkin Muffins

Servings:6
Cooking Time: 9 Minutes

Ingredients:
- 1 ¼ cups all-purpose flour
- 2 teaspoons baking powder
- ½ teaspoon baking soda
- 1 teaspoon pumpkin pie spice
- ⅛ teaspoon salt
- ¼ cup pumpkin purée
- ½ teaspoon vanilla extract
- 1 tablespoon unsalted butter, melted

- 2 large eggs
- ⅓ cup packed light brown sugar
- 1 cup water

Directions:
1. Grease six silicone cupcake liners.

2. In a large bowl, combine flour, baking powder, baking soda, pumpkin pie spice, and salt.

3. In a medium bowl, combine pumpkin purée, vanilla, butter, eggs, and brown sugar.

4. Pour wet ingredients from medium bowl into large bowl with dry ingredients. Gently combine ingredients. Do not overmix. Spoon mixture into prepared cupcake liners.

5. Add water to the Instant Pot and insert steam rack. Place cupcake liners on top. Lock lid.

6. Press the Manual or Pressure Cook button and adjust time to 9 minutes. When timer beeps, quick-release pressure until float valve drops. Unlock lid.

7. Remove muffins from pot and set aside to cool 30 minutes. Serve.

Banana & Vanilla Pancakes

Servings: 6
Cooking Time: 15 Minutes

Ingredients:
- 2 bananas, mashed
- 1 ¼ cups milk
- 2 eggs
- 1 ½ cups rolled oats
- 1 ½ tsp baking powder
- 1 tsp vanilla extract
- 2 tsp coconut oil
- 1 tbsp honey

Directions:
1. Combine the bananas, milk, eggs, oats, baking powder, vanilla, coconut oil, and honey in a blender and pulse until a completely smooth batter. Grease the inner pot with cooking spray. Spread 1 spoon batter at the bottom. Cook for 2 minutes on Sauté, flip the crepe, and cook for another minute. Repeat the process with the remaining batter. Serve immediately with your favorite topping.

Spinach & Feta Pie With Cherry Tomatoes

Servings: 2
Cooking Time: 35 Minutes

Ingredients:
- 4 eggs
- Salt and pepper to taste
- ½ cup heavy cream
- 1 cup cherry tomatoes, halved
- 1 cup baby spinach
- 1 spring onion, chopped
- ¼ cup feta, crumbled
- 1 tbsp parsley, chopped

Directions:
1. Grease a baking dish with cooking spray and add in the spinach and onion. In a bowl, whisk the eggs, heavy cream, salt, and pepper. Pour over the spinach and arrange the cherry tomato on top. Sprinkle with the feta.
2. Add a cup of water to the Instant Pot and insert a trivet. Place the dish on the trivet. Seal the lid, press Manual, and cook on High pressure for 15 minutes. Release pressure naturally for 10 minutes. Scatter parsley to serve.

French Cheese & Spinach Quiche

Servings: 5
Cooking Time: 20 Minutes

Ingredients:
- 1 lb spinach, chopped
- ½ cup mascarpone cheese
- ½ cup feta cheese, shredded
- 3 eggs, beaten
- ½ cup goat cheese
- 3 tbsp butter
- ½ cup milk
- 1 pack pie dough

Directions:
1. In a bowl, mix spinach, eggs, mascarpone, feta and goat cheeses. Dust a clean surface with flour and unfold the pie sheets onto it. Using a rolling pin, roll the dough to fit your Instant Pot. Repeat with the other sheets. Combine milk and butter in a skillet. Bring to a boil and melt the butter completely. Remove from the heat.
2. Grease a baking pan with oil. Place in 2 pie sheets and brush with milk mixture. Make the first layer of spinach mixture and cover with another two pie sheets. Again, brush with butter and milk mixture, and repeat until you have used all ingredients. Pour 1 cup water into your Instant Pot

and insert a trivet. Lower the pan on the trivet. Seal the lid. Cook on High Pressure for 6 minutes. Do a quick release. Place parchment paper under the pie to use it as a lifting method to remove the pie. Serve cold.

Tofu Hash Brown Breakfast

Servings: 4
Cooking Time: 21 Minutes

Ingredients:
- 1 cup tofu cubes
- 2 cups frozen hash browns
- 8 beaten eggs
- 1 cup shredded cheddar
- ¼ cup milk
- Salt and pepper to taste

Directions:
1. Set your Instant Pot to Sauté. Place in tofu and cook until browned on all sides, about 4 minutes. Add in hash brown and cook for 2 minutes. Beat eggs, cheddar cheese, milk, salt, and pepper in a bowl and pour over hash brown. Seal the lid, select Manual, and cook for 5 minutes on High. Once done, perform a quick pressure release. Cut into slices before serving.

Light & Fruity Yogurt

Servings: 12
Cooking Time: 24hr

Ingredients:
- ¼ cup Greek yogurt containing active cultures
- 1 lb raspberries, mashed
- 1 cup sugar
- 3 tbsp gelatin
- 1 tbsp fresh orange juice
- 8 cups milk

Directions:
1. In a bowl, add sugar and raspberries and stir well to dissolve the sugar. Let sit for 30 minutes at room temperature. Add in orange juice and gelatin and mix well until dissolved. Remove the mixture and place in a sealable container, close, and allow to sit for 12 hrs to 24 hrs at room temperature before placing in the fridge. Refrigerate for a maximum of 2 weeks.
2. Into the cooker, add milk, and close the lid. The steam vent should be set to Venting then to Sealing. Select Yogurt until "Boil" is showed on display. When complete, there will be a display of "Yogurt" on the screen.
3. Open the lid and using a food thermometer, ensure the milk temperature is at least 185°F. Transfer the steel pot to

a wire rack and allow to cool for 30 minutes until the milk has reached 110°F.

4. In a bowl, mix ½ cup warm milk and yogurt. Transfer the mixture into the remaining warm milk and stir without having to scrape the steel pot's bottom. Take the steel pot back to the base of the pot and seal the lid.

5. Select Yogurt and cook for 8 hrs. Allow the yogurt to chill in a refrigerator for 1-2 hrs. Transfer the chilled yogurt to a bowl and stir in fresh raspberry jam.

Strawberry Jam

Servings: 6
Cooking Time: 30 Minutes

Ingredients:
- 1 lb strawberries, chopped
- 1 cup sugar
- ½ lemon, juiced and zested
- 1 tbsp mint, chopped

Directions:
1. Add the strawberries, sugar, lemon juice, and zest to the Instant Pot. Seal the lid, select manual, and cook for 2 minutes on High.

2. Release pressure naturally for 10 minutes. Open the lid and stir in chopped mint. Select Sauté and continue cooking until the jam thickens, about 10 minutes. Let to cool before serving.

Greek Yogurt With Honey & Walnuts

Servings: 10
Cooking Time: 15hr

Ingredients:
- 2 tbsp Greek yogurt
- 8 cups milk
- ¼ cup sugar honey
- 1 tsp vanilla extract
- 1 cup walnuts, chopped

Directions:
1. Add the milk to your Instant Pot. Seal the lid and press Yogurt until the display shows "Boil". When the cooking cycle is over, the display will show Yogurt. Open the lid and check that milk temperature is at least 175°F. Get rid of the skin lying on the milk's surface. Let cool in an ice bath until it becomes warm to the touch.

2. In a bowl, mix one cup of milk and yogurt to make a smooth consistency. Mix the milk with yogurt mixture. Transfer to the pot and place on your Pressure cooker.

3. Seal the lid, press Yogurt, and adjust the timer to 9 hrs. Once cooking is complete, strain the yogurt into a bowl us-

ing a strainer with cheesecloth. Chill for 4 hours.

4. Add in vanilla and honey and gently stir well. Spoon the yogurt into glass jars. Serve sprinkled with walnuts and enjoy.

Chicken Sandwiches With Barbecue Sauce

Servings: 4
Cooking Time: 50 Minutes

Ingredients:
- 4 chicken thighs, boneless and skinless
- 2 cups barbecue sauce
- 1 onion, minced
- 2 garlic cloves, minced
- 2 tbsp minced fresh parsley
- 1 tbsp lemon juice
- 1 tbsp mayonnaise
- 2 cups lettuce, shredded
- 4 burger buns

Directions:
1. Into the pot, place the garlic, onion, and barbecue sauce. Add in the chicken and toss it to coat. Seal the lid and cook on High Pressure for 15 minutes. Do a natural release for 10 minutes. Use two forks to shred the chicken and mix it into the sauce. Press Keep Warm and let the mixture simmer for 15 minutes to thicken the sauce until the desired consistency.

2. In a bowl, mix lemon juice, mayonnaise, and parsley; toss lettuce into the mixture to coat. Separate the chicken into equal parts to match the burger buns; top with lettuce and complete the sandwiches.

Buckwheat Pancake With Yogurt & Berries

Servings: 4
Cooking Time: 15 Minutes

Ingredients:
- 1 cup buckwheat flour
- 2 tsp baking powder
- 1 ¼ cups milk
- 1 egg
- 1 tsp vanilla sugar
- 1 tsp strawberry extract
- 1 cup Greek yogurt
- 1 cup fresh berries

Directions:

1. In a bowl, whisk milk and egg until foamy. Gradually add flour and continue to beat until combined. Add baking powder, strawberry extract, and vanilla sugar. Spoon the batter in a greased cake pan. Pour 1 cup of water into the pot. Place a trivet. Lay the pan on the trivet. Seal the lid and cook for 5 minutes on High Pressure. Do a quick release. Top pancake with yogurt and berries.

Lazy Steel Cut Oats With Coconut

Servings: 2
Cooking Time: 25 Minutes

Ingredients:
- 1 tsp coconut oil
- 1 cup steel-cut oats
- ¾ cup coconut milk
- ¼ cup sugar
- ½ tsp vanilla extract
- 1 tbsp shredded coconut

Directions:
1. Warm coconut oil on Sauté in your Instant Pot. Add oats and cook as you stir until soft and toasted. Add in milk, sugar, vanilla, and 2 cups water and stir. Seal the lid and press Porridge. Cook for 12 minutes on High Pressure. Set steam vent to Venting to release the pressure quickly. Open the lid. Add oats as you stir to mix any extra liquid. Top with coconut and serve.

Smoked Salmon & Egg Muffins

Servings: 2
Cooking Time: 15 Minutes

Ingredients:
- 4 beaten eggs
- 2 salmon slices, chopped
- 4 tbsp mozzarella, shredded
- 1 green onion, chopped

Directions:
1. Beat eggs, salmon, mozzarella cheese, and onion in a bowl. Share into ramekins. Pour 1 cup of water into your Instant Pot and fit in a trivet.
2. Place the tins on top of the trivet and seal the lid. Select Manual and cook for 8 minutes on High pressure. Once done, let sit for 2 minutes, then perform a quick pressure release and unlock the lid. Serve immediately.

Lemony Pancake Bites With Blueberry Syrup

Servings:4
Cooking Time: 24 Minutes

Ingredients:
- 1 packet Hungry Jack buttermilk pancake mix
- ⅔ cup whole milk
- Juice and zest of ½ medium lemon
- ⅛ teaspoon salt
- 1 cup water
- ½ cup blueberry syrup

Directions:
1. Grease a seven-hole silicone egg mold.
2. In a medium bowl, combine pancake mix, milk, lemon juice and zest, and salt. Fill egg mold with half of batter.
3. Add water to the Instant Pot and insert steam rack. Place filled egg mold on steam rack. Lock lid.
4. Press the Manual or Pressure Cook button and adjust time to 12 minutes. When timer beeps, quick-release pressure until float valve drops. Unlock lid.
5. Allow pancake bites to cool, about 3 minutes until cool enough to handle. Pop out of mold. Repeat with remaining batter.
6. Serve warm with syrup for dipping.

Chapter 3 Appetizers, Soups & Sides

Chorizo Soup With Roasted Tomatoes

Servings: 6
Cooking Time: 25 Minutes

Ingredients:
- 28 oz fire-roasted diced tomatoes
- 3 tbsp olive oil
- 2 shallots, chopped
- 3 cloves garlic, minced
- Salt and pepper to taste
- 4 cups beef broth
- ½ cup tomatoes, chopped
- ½ cup raw cashews
- 1 tbsp red wine vinegar
- 3 chorizo sausage, chopped
- ½ cup chopped basil

Directions:
1. Warm oil on Sauté and cook chorizo until crispy. Remove to a plate lined with paper towels. Add in garlic and shallots and cook for 5 minutes until soft. Season with salt. Stir in red wine vinegar, broth, fire-roasted tomatoes, cashews, tomatoes, and pepper into the cooker. Seal the lid and cook on High Pressure for 8 minutes. Release the pressure quickly. Pour the soup into a blender and process until smooth. Divide into bowls. Top with chorizo and decorate with basil.

Broccoli-gruyère Soup

Servings:4
Cooking Time: 15 Minutes

Ingredients:
- 1 large bunch broccoli, coarsely chopped
- 1 medium sweet onion, peeled and chopped
- 4 cups chicken broth
- 1 teaspoon salt
- ½ teaspoon ground black pepper
- ⅛ teaspoon ground nutmeg
- ½ cup heavy cream
- 1 cup shredded sharp Gruyère cheese

Directions:
1. In the Instant Pot, add broccoli, onion, broth, salt, pepper, and nutmeg. Lock lid.
2. Press the Manual or Pressure Cook button and adjust time to 15 minutes. When timer beeps, quick-release pressure until float valve drops. Unlock lid.
3. Add cream and cheese. In the Instant Pot, purée the soup with an immersion blender, or use a stand blender and purée in batches until desired consistency is reached.
4. Ladle soup into bowls. Serve warm.

Garbanzo Stew With Onions & Tomatoes

Servings: 5
Cooking Time: 35 Minutes

Ingredients:
- 1 lb chickpeas, soaked
- 3 purple onions, chopped
- 2 tomatoes, chopped
- 2 oz fresh parsley, chopped
- 3 cups vegetable broth
- 1 tbsp paprika
- 2 tbsp olive oil

Directions:
1. Warm olive oil on Sauté and stir-fry the onions for 3 minutes. Add chickpeas, tomatoes, broth, parsley, and paprika. Seal the lid and cook on the Meat/Stew for 30 minutes on High. Do a quick release. Serve warm.

Savory Butternut Squash Soup

Servings:6
Cooking Time: 25 Minutes

Ingredients:
- 1 tablespoon olive oil
- 1 small onion, peeled and diced
- 2 celery stalks, sliced
- 3 pounds butternut squash, peeled, seeded, and cubed
- 1 small Granny Smith apple, peeled, cored, and diced
- 1 teaspoon sea salt
- ¼ teaspoon white pepper
- 1 teaspoon celery seed
- ¼ teaspoon ground nutmeg
- ¼ teaspoon hot sauce
- 1" piece of fresh ginger, peeled and minced
- 4 cups chicken broth

Directions:
1. Press the Sauté button on the Instant Pot and heat the oil. Add the onion and celery. Sauté for 5 minutes until onions are translucent. Add the butternut squash and apple. Continue to sauté for 2–3 minutes until apples are tender. Add remaining ingredients. Lock lid.
2. Press the Manual button and adjust time to 15 minutes. When timer beeps, quick-release pressure until float valve drops and then unlock lid.
3. In the Instant Pot, purée soup with an immersion blender, or use a stand blender and purée in batches. Ladle into bowls and serve warm.

Frittata With Vegetables & Cheese

Servings: 4
Cooking Time: 30 Minutes

Ingredients:
- 4 eggs
- 8 oz spinach, finely chopped
- ½ cup cheddar, shredded
- ½ cup ricotta, crumbled
- 3 cherry tomatoes, halved
- ¼ cup bell pepper, chopped
- 1 cup chopped broccoli
- 4 tbsp olive oil
- Salt and pepper to taste
- ¼ tsp dried oregano
- 2 tsp celery leaves, chopped

Directions:
1. Heat olive oil on Sauté. Add spinach and cook for 5 minutes, stirring occasionally. Add tomatoes, peppers, and broccoli and stir-fry for 3-4 more minutes. In a bowl, Whisk eggs, cheddar cheese, and ricotta cheese. Pour in the pot and cook for 5-7 minutes. Season with salt, black pepper, and oregano; press Cancel. Serve with celery.

Mushroom-potato Hash Casserole

Servings: 4
Cooking Time: 20 Minutes

Ingredients:
- 1 onion, chopped
- 2 garlic cloves, minced
- 1 lb potatoes, peeled
- 1 cup mushrooms, sliced
- Salt and pepper to taste
- ½ tsp paprika
- ½ tsp porcini powder
- ¼ tsp chili pepper powder

Directions:
1. Place the potatoes in your Instant Pot and cover them with water. Seal the lid, select Manual, and cook for 5 minutes on High. Perform a quick pressure release. Unlock the lid. Remove the potatoes with a slotted spoon, then shred them with a cheese grater into a bowl.
2. Add in the mushrooms, garlic, onion, paprika, porcini powder, chili pepper powder, salt, and pepper and stir to combine. Transfer the mixture to a greased baking dish. Insert a trivet in the pot over the potato water and place the dish on the trivet. Seal the lid, select Manual, and cook for 7 minutes. Perform a quick pressure release.

Classic Palak Paneer Dip

Servings: 4
Cooking Time: 15 Minutes

Ingredients:
- ¼ cup milk
- 2 tsp butter
- 1 tsp cumin seeds
- 1 tsp coriander seeds
- 1 tomato, chopped
- 1 tsp minced fresh ginger
- 1 tsp minced fresh garlic
- 1 red onion, chopped
- 1 lb spinach, chopped
- 1 tsp salt
- 2 cups paneer, cubed
- 1 tsp chili powder

Directions:
1. Warm butter in your Instant Pot on Sauté. Add in onion, garlic, cumin seeds, coriander, chili powder, and ginger and fry for 1 minute. Add in salt, 1 cup water, and spinach. Seal the lid and cook for 1 minute on High Pressure. Release the pressure quickly. Add spinach mixture to a blender and pulse until smooth. Transfer to a bowl. Mix in the paneer, milk, and tomato. Serve warm.

Kimchi Ramen Noodle Soup

Servings: 4
Cooking Time: 20 Minutes

Ingredients:
- 1 chicken breast, cubed
- 2 tbsp olive oil
- ½ tsp ground ginger
- 2 tbsp garlic, minced
- 4 cups chicken stock
- 2 tbsp soy sauce
- ½ tbsp kimchi paste
- 1 cup mushrooms, chopped
- 10 oz ramen noodles
- 1 lb collard greens, trimmed
- 2 tbsp cilantro, chopped
- 1 red chili, chopped to serve

Directions:
1. Warm the olive oil on Sauté. Add in the chicken and cook for 5-6 minutes until slightly browned. Add in the mushrooms, garlic, kimchi paste, and ginger and sauté for 4-5 minutes. Mix in chicken stock and soy sauce. Seal the lid and cook on High Pressure for 10 minutes. Release pressure quickly. Press Sauté and stir in the ramen noodles and collard greens and simmer for 2 minutes. Top with red chili and cilantro to serve.

Dilled Salmon Soup

Servings: 2
Cooking Time: 20 Minutes

Ingredients:
- ¼ cup chopped green tomatoes
- ½ lb salmon fillet
- 1 cup fresh dill
- 2 tsp sliced shallots
- 1 tsp sliced garlic
- ¼ tsp ginger
- ¼ tsp tamarind
- 1 tbsp lemon juice
- 1 cup water
- 1 bay leaf
- ½ tsp salt

Directions:
1. Slice salmon fillet into medium dices and place them in your Instant Pot. Add in water, green tomatoes, fresh dill, shallot, garlic, ginger, bay leaf, salt, tamarind, and lemon juice. Seal the lid, select Soup, and cook for 4 minutes on High. When done, allow a natural release for 10 minutes and unlock the lid. Serve warm and enjoy!

Gingered Sweet Potatoes

Servings:6
Cooking Time: 10 Minutes

Ingredients:
- 2½ pounds sweet potatoes, peeled and diced large
- 2 cups water
- 1 tablespoon minced fresh ginger
- ½ teaspoon sea salt
- 1 tablespoon pure maple syrup
- 1 tablespoon butter
- ¼ cup milk

Directions:
1. Add potatoes and water to Instant Pot. Lock lid.
2. Press the Manual button and adjust time to 10 minutes. When the timer beeps, let the pressure release naturally until the float valve drops and then unlock lid.
3. Drain water from the Instant Pot. Add remaining ingredients to the potatoes. Using an immersion blender directly in the Instant Pot, cream the potatoes until desired consistency. Serve warm.

Simple Onion Cheese Soup

Servings: 4
Cooking Time: 10 Minutes

Ingredients:
- 1 onion, chopped
- 2 tbsp all-purpose flour
- 4 cups vegetable broth
- 2 cups Monterey Jack, grated
- 2 cups milk
- 2 tbsp butter

Directions:
1. Melt butter on Sauté and cook the onion and flour for 2 minutes. Gradually stir in the broth and milk. Seal the lid. Cook on High Pressure for 5 minutes. Do a quick pressure release. Stir in cheese until melted. Serve.

Aromatic Lamb Stew

Servings: 4
Cooking Time: 60 Minutes

Ingredients:
- 1 ½ lb lamb stew meat, cubed
- 2 tbsp olive oil
- 3 garlic cloves, chopped
- 1 onion, chopped
- 3 cups mushrooms, sliced
- 1 celery stalk, chopped
- 1 carrot, chopped
- 28 oz canned tomatoes, diced
- 3 cups chicken broth
- ½ cup pomegranate juice
- ½ tsp allspice
- 1 tsp ground cumin
- ½ tsp ground bay leaf
- ½ tsp curry powder
- 1 tsp ground coriander
- Salt and pepper to taste

Directions:
1. In a bowl, mix the allspice, ground cumin, ground bay leaf, curry powder, ground coriander, salt, and pepper and add in the lamb; toss to coat. Warm the olive oil in your Instant Pot on Sauté. Add in the lamb and cook for 5-6 minutes until browned. Add in garlic, onion, celery, carrot, and mushrooms and sauté for 5 minutes. Pour in tomatoes, pomegranate juice, and chicken broth.
2. Seal the lid, select Manual, and cook for 30 minutes on High pressure. When over, allow a natural release for 10 minutes, then perform a quick pressure release. Serve.

Pea & Garbanzo Bean Soup

Servings: 4
Cooking Time: 30 Minutes

Ingredients:
- 2 tbsp olive oil
- ½ cup shallots, sliced
- 14 oz can garbanzo beans
- ½ cup green peas
- 2 Roma chopped tomatoes
- 4 cups vegetable broth
- Salt and pepper to taste
- 1 lemon, zested and juiced

Directions:
1. Warm the olive oil in your Instant Pot on Sauté. Add in shallots and cook for 3 minutes until tender and fragrant. Pour in vegetable broth, tomatoes, lemon zest, and garbanzo beans and stir.
2. Seal the lid, select Manual, and cook for 10 minutes on High pressure. Once over, allow a natural release for 10 minutes, then perform a quick pressure release and unlock the lid. Stir in green peas and let it sit covered in the residual heat until warmed through. Season with salt and pepper and drizzle with lemon juice. Serve.

Wild Mushroom Soup

Servings:4
Cooking Time: 25 Minutes

Ingredients:
- 3 tablespoons unsalted butter
- 1 small sweet onion, peeled and diced
- 2 cups sliced mushrooms (shiitake, cremini, portobello, etc.)
- 4 cups chicken broth
- 1 tablespoon Italian seasoning
- 1 teaspoon salt
- ½ teaspoon ground black pepper
- 1 cup heavy cream
- 2 teaspoons cooking sherry

Directions:
1. Press the Sauté button on the Instant Pot. Add butter and heat until melted, then add onion. Sauté 3–5 minutes until onions are translucent.
2. Add mushrooms, broth, Italian seasoning, salt, and pepper. Press the Cancel button. Lock lid.
3. Press the Soup button and adjust time to 20 minutes. When timer beeps, let pressure release naturally for 10 minutes. Quick-release any additional pressure until float valve drops. Unlock lid.

4. Add cream and sherry. Use an immersion blender directly in pot to blend soup until desired consistency is reached, either chunky or smooth.
5. Ladle soup into bowls. Serve warm.

Creamy Chicken Soup

Servings:4
Cooking Time: 25 Minutes

Ingredients:
- 1 pound bone-in chicken thighs, cut in ½" cubes (save bones)
- 1 teaspoon salt
- ½ teaspoon ground black pepper
- 2 tablespoons unsalted butter
- 1 small yellow onion, peeled and diced
- 1 large carrot, peeled and diced
- 4 cups chicken broth
- 1 tablespoon Italian seasoning
- ½ cup heavy cream

Directions:
1. Season chicken with salt and pepper.
2. Press the Sauté button on the Instant Pot. Add butter and heat until melted. Add chicken, onion, and carrot. Sauté 3–5 minutes until onions are translucent. Add broth, Italian seasoning, and chicken bones. Press the Cancel button. Lock lid.
3. Press the Soup button and adjust time to 20 minutes. When timer beeps, let pressure release naturally for 10 minutes. Quick-release any additional pressure until float valve drops. Unlock lid. Remove and discard chicken bones.
4. Stir in cream. Ladle soup into bowls. Serve warm.

Milk-boiled Corn On The Cob

Servings:8
Cooking Time: 2 Minutes

Ingredients:
- 1 cup whole milk
- ½ cup water
- 4 fresh ears corn, shucked and halved
- 1 teaspoon salt
- 3 tablespoons unsalted butter, cut into 4 pats

Directions:
1. Add milk, water, and corn to the Instant Pot. Sprinkle with salt and place butter pats on corn. Lock lid.
2. Press the Manual or Pressure Cook button and adjust time to 2 minutes. When timer beeps, quick-release pressure until float valve drops. Unlock lid. Toss corn twice in pot liquids.

3. Transfer corn to a platter. Serve warm.

Broccoli & Mushroom Egg Cups

Servings: 6
Cooking Time: 15 Minutes

Ingredients:
- 1 tsp dried oregano
- 10 eggs
- 1 cup Pecorino cheese, grated
- 1 cup heavy cream
- 4 oz broccoli florets
- 1 onion, chopped
- 1 cup sliced mushrooms
- 1 tbsp chopped parsley
- Salt and pepper to taste

Directions:
1. Pour 1 cup of water into your Instant Pot and fit in a trivet. In a bowl, whisk the eggs and heavy cream. Mix in Pecorino cheese, broccoli, onion, oregano, mushrooms, parsley, salt, and black pepper. Divide the egg mixture between small jars and seal the lids. Place them on the trivet and seal the lid. Select Manual and cook for 5 minutes on High pressure. When done, perform a quick pressure release and unlock the lid. Remove the jars carefully and serve.

Potatoes & Tuna Salad With Pickles

Servings: 4
Cooking Time: 15 Minutes

Ingredients:
- ½ cup pimento-stuffed green olives
- ½ cup chopped roasted red peppers
- 1 lb potatoes, quartered
- 2 eggs
- 3 tbsp melted butter
- Salt and pepper to taste
- 6 pickles, chopped
- 2 tbsp red wine vinegar
- 10 oz canned tuna, drained

Directions:
1. Pour 2 cups of water into the pot and add potatoes. Place a trivet over the potatoes. Lay the eggs on the trivet. Seal the lid and cook for 8 minutes on High Pressure. Do a quick release. Drain and remove potatoes to a bowl.
2. Fill a bowl with ice water. Add in the eggs to cool. Drizzle melted butter over the potatoes and season with salt and pepper. Peel and chop the chilled eggs. Add pickles, eggs, peppers, tuna, and red wine vinegar to the potatoes and mix to coat. Serve topped with olives. Enjoy!

Moroccan Lentil Soup

Servings: 4
Cooking Time: 30 Minutes

Ingredients:
- 2 tsp olive oil
- 2 garlic cloves, minced
- 1 onion, chopped
- 1 cup red lentils
- 2 tbsp tomato purée
- 1 potato, chopped
- 1 carrot, chopped
- ½ cup celery
- ½ tsp ground coriander
- ½ tsp ground cumin
- ½ tsp cinnamon
- 1 red chili pepper, chopped
- 4 cups water
- Salt and pepper to taste
- 2 tbsp fresh mint, chopped

Directions:
1. Warm olive oil in your Instant Pot on Sauté. Add in garlic, celery, carrot, and onion and cook for 3 minutes. Stir in chili pepper, tomato puree, ground coriander, cumin, salt, pepper, and cinnamon and cook for 1 minute. Pour in lentils, potato, and 4 cups of water and stir.
2. Seal the lid, select Manual, and cook for 10 minutes on High pressure. When done, allow a natural release for 10 minutes and unlock the lid. Sprinkle with mint and serve.

Chowder With Broccoli, Carrot & Tofu

Servings: 4
Cooking Time: 35 Minutes

Ingredients:
- 1 head broccoli, chopped
- 1 carrot, chopped
- 2 tbsp sesame oil
- 1 onion, chopped
- 2 garlic cloves
- 1 cup soy milk
- 2 cups vegetable broth
- ¼ cup tofu, crumbled
- A pinch of salt

Directions:
1. Heat oil on Sauté. Add onion and garlic and stir-fry for 2 minutes, or until translucent. Pour in broth, a cup of water, broccoli, salt, and carrot. Seal the lid and cook on Manual/

Pressure Cook for 5 minutes on High. Do a quick release. Stir in the soy milk and transfer to a food processor. Pulse until creamy. Serve with crumbled tofu.

Loaded Broccoli

Servings:4
Cooking Time: 0 Minutes

Ingredients:
- 1 cup water
- 1 medium head broccoli, chopped
- ½ teaspoon salt
- 1 cup shredded sharp Cheddar cheese
- ⅓ cup sour cream
- 4 slices bacon, cooked and crumbled
- 2 tablespoons chopped fresh chives

Directions:
1. Add water to the Instant Pot and insert steamer basket. Arrange broccoli in basket in an even layer. Lock lid.
2. Press the Steam button and adjust time to 0 minutes. When timer beeps, quick-release pressure until float valve drops. Unlock lid.
3. Remove steamer basket. Transfer broccoli to a serving dish and season with salt. Top with cheese. Garnish with sour cream, bacon, and chives. Serve.

Rosemary Potato Fries

Servings: 4
Cooking Time: 15 Minutes

Ingredients:
- 1 lb potatoes, cut into ½ inch sticks
- Sea salt to taste
- 4 tbsp olive oil
- 2 tbsp rosemary, chopped

Directions:
1. Place 1 cup of water in your Instant Pot and fit in a steamer basket. Place the potatoes in the basket and seal the lid. Select Manual and cook for 3 minutes on High.
2. Once ready, perform a quick pressure release. Unlock the lid. Remove potatoes to a bowl and pat them dry.
3. Discard the water and dry the pot. Warm the olive oil in the pot on Sauté. Place the potato sticks and cook until golden brown. Sprinkle with salt and rosemary to serve.

Lentil Pâté

Servings: 10
Cooking Time: 20 Minutes

Ingredients:
- 2 tablespoons olive oil
- 1 small onion, peeled and diced
- 1 celery stalk, diced
- 3 cloves garlic, minced
- 2 cups dried lentils
- 4 cups water
- 1 teaspoon red wine vinegar
- 2 tablespoons tomato paste
- 1 teaspoon ground coriander
- 1 teaspoon ground cumin
- 1 teaspoon sea salt
- 1 teaspoon ground black pepper

Directions:
1. Press Sauté button on Instant Pot. Heat oil and add onions and celery. Stir-fry for 3–5 minutes until the onions are translucent. Add garlic. Cook for an additional minute. Add remaining ingredients. Lock lid.
2. Press the Manual button and adjust time to 15 minutes. When the timer beeps, let the pressure release naturally for 10 minutes.
3. Quick-release any additional pressure until float valve drops and then unlock lid. Transfer ingredients to a blender or food processor and process until smooth. Spoon into a serving bowl and serve.

Quick Chicken Soup

Servings: 4
Cooking Time: 25 Minutes

Ingredients:
- ½ cup mushrooms, chopped
- ½ lb Chicken Breasts
- 2 tbsp Olive oil
- 1 large Carrot, chopped
- 1 Celery Stalk, chopped
- 1 onion, chopped
- 2 garlic cloves, minced
- 1 Green Chili Pepper, sliced
- Salt and pepper to taste
- 2 cups Chicken Broth

Directions:
1. Warm olive oil in your Instant Pot on Sauté. Place the carrot, celery, onion, garlic, salt, pepper, and green chili pepper and cook for 3 minutes. Mix in broth, chicken breasts, mushrooms, and 2 cups of water. Seal the lid, select Soup, and cook for 10 minutes on High. Do a quick pressure release. Remove the chicken, shred it, and back it to the pot. Cook for 3 minutes on Sauté and serve.

Simple Carrot & Oregano Soup

Servings: 4
Cooking Time: 30 Minutes

Ingredients:
- 2 carrots, chopped
- 4 cups vegetable broth
- 1 tbsp butter
- ½ tsp dried oregano
- ½ tsp salt

Directions:
1. Add carrots, broth, butter, oregano, and salt to the pot. Seal the lid and cook on Manual/Pressure Cook for 12 minutes on High. Do a natural release for 10 minutes. Transfer to a food processor and pulse until creamy.

Broccoli & Egg Salad

Servings: 4
Cooking Time: 20 Minutes

Ingredients:
- 1 lb small broccoli florets
- 4 large eggs
- 1 cup mayonnaise
- 2 tbsp parsley, chopped
- ¼ cup onion, chopped
- 1 tbsp dill pickle juice
- 1 tbsp yellow mustard
- Salt and pepper to taste

Directions:
1. Pour 1 cup water into your Instant Pot and fit in a trivet. Place broccoli and eggs on the trivet. Seal the lid, select Manual, and cook for 5 minutes on High. When over, perform a quick pressure release. Remove the eggs and transfer to a bowl with cold water for 2-3 minutes.
2. Meanwhile, mix mayonnaise, parsley, onion, dill pickle juice, and mustard in a bowl. Sprinkle with salt and pepper. Peel and slice the eggs. Place sliced egg and broccoli into mayonnaise mixture and toss to coat. Serve.

Pizza-style Stuffed Mushrooms

Servings:4
Cooking Time: 2 Minutes

Ingredients:
- ¼ cup jarred pizza sauce
- 8 ounces whole baby bella mushrooms, stems removed
- ½ cup shredded mozzarella
- ¼ cup small-diced pepperoni
- 1 cup water
- 5 fresh basil leaves, julienned

Directions:
1. Spoon pizza sauce evenly into mushroom caps to cover bottoms. Top with mozzarella cheese and then pepperoni.
2. Pour water into the Instant Pot. Place stuffed mushrooms in steamer basket, then insert basket in pot. Lock lid.
3. Press the Manual or Pressure Cook button and adjust time to 2 minutes. Adjust pressure to Low. When timer beeps, quick-release pressure until float valve drops. Unlock lid.
4. Transfer mushrooms to a serving dish. Garnish with basil. Serve warm.

Rustic Soup With Turkey Balls & Carrots

Servings: 4
Cooking Time: 45 Minutes

Ingredients:
- 2 tbsp olive oil
- 6 oz turkey balls
- 4 cups chicken broth
- 1 onion, chopped
- 1 garlic clove, minced
- 3 large carrots, chopped
- Salt and pepper to taste
- 1 tbsp cilantro, chopped

Directions:
1. Heat olive oil on Sauté and stir-fry onion, carrots, and garlic for 5 minutes until soft. Add turkey balls, broth, salt, and pepper to the pot. Seal the lid and press Manual. Cook for 25 minutes on HIgh. Release the pressure naturally for 10 minutes and serve sprinkled with cilantro.

Chapter 4 Poultry

Creamy Pesto Chicken

Servings: 6
Cooking Time: 10 Minutes

Ingredients:
- ½ cup pesto
- ¾ cup heavy cream
- 1 tablespoon all-purpose flour
- 2 tablespoons grated Parmesan cheese
- 2 cloves garlic, peeled and minced
- ¼ teaspoon salt
- ½ teaspoon ground black pepper
- 3 pounds boneless and skinless chicken thighs
- 1 cup water

Directions:
1. In a medium bowl, whisk together pesto, cream, flour, cheese, garlic, salt, and pepper.
2. Add chicken to a 7-cup glass baking dish. Pour pesto mixture over chicken.
3. Add water to the Instant Pot and insert steam rack. Place glass baking dish on steam rack. Lock lid.
4. Press the Manual or Pressure Cook button and adjust time to 10 minutes. When timer beeps, let pressure release naturally for 10 minutes. Quick-release any additional pressure until float valve drops. Unlock lid. Check chicken using a meat thermometer to ensure internal temperature is at least 165°F.
5. Carefully remove dish from pot. Serve warm.

Spring Onion Buffalo Wings

Servings: 6
Cooking Time: 30 Minutes

Ingredients:
- 2 lb chicken wings, sectioned
- 2 spring onions, sliced diagonally
- ½ cup hot pepper sauce
- 1 tbsp Worcestershire sauce
- 3 tbsp butter
- Sea salt to taste
- 2 tbsp sugar, light brown

Directions:
1. Combine hot sauce, Worcestershire sauce, butter, salt, and brown sugar in a bowl and microwave for 20 seconds until the butter melts. Pour 1 cup of water into your Instant Pot and fit in a trivet. Place the chicken wings on the trivet and seal the lid. Select Manual and cook for 10 minutes on High pressure.
2. Once done, perform a quick pressure release and unlock the lid. Remove chicken wings to a baking dish and brush the top with marinade. Broil for 4-5 minutes, turn the wings and brush more marinade. Broil for 4-5 minutes more. Top with spring onions and serve.

Chicken & Zucchini Pilaf

Servings: 4
Cooking Time: 25 Minutes

Ingredients:
- 1 lb boneless, skinless chicken legs
- 2 tsp olive oil
- 1 zucchini, chopped
- 1 cup leeks, chopped
- 2 garlic cloves, minced
- 1 tbsp chopped rosemary
- 2 tsp chopped fresh thyme
- Salt and pepper to taste
- 2 cups chicken stock
- 1 cup rice, rinsed

Directions:
1. Warm oil on Sauté in your Instant Pot. Add in zucchini and cook for 5 minutes. Stir in thyme, leeks, rosemary, pepper, salt, and garlic. Cook the mixture for 4 minutes. Add in ½ cup chicken stock to deglaze, scrape the bottom to get rid of any browned bits of food.
2. When liquid stops simmering, add in the remaining stock, rice, and chicken with more pepper and salt. Seal the lid and cook on High Pressure for 5 minutes. Do a quick release. Carefully open the lid. Serve warm.

Saucy Chicken Marsala

Servings: 4
Cooking Time: 30 Minutes

Ingredients:
- 4 chicken breasts
- ¼ cup ketchup
- ¾ cup Marsala wine
- ½ cup soy sauce
- 2 green onions, chopped

Directions:
1. Place chicken breasts, 1 cup of water, ketchup, Marsala wine, and soy sauce in your Instant Pot and stir. Seal the lid and cook for 15 minutes on Manual.
2. When ready, perform a quick pressure release and unlock the lid. Simmer for 5 minutes on Sauté until the sauce thickens. Top with green onions and serve.

Hot Chicken With Coriander & Ginger

Servings: 6
Cooking Time: 45 Minutes

Ingredients:
- 2 lb chicken thighs
- 1 tbsp ancho chili powder
- 1 tsp fresh basil
- Salt and pepper to taste
- 6 cups chicken broth
- 1 tbsp ginger, freshly grated
- 1 tbsp coriander seeds
- 3 garlic cloves, crushed

Directions:
1. Season the chicken with chili powder, salt, and pepper and place in the Instant Pot. Add the chicken broth broth, ginger, garlic, and coriander seeds; stir. Seal the lid and cook on Meat/Stew for 25 minutes on High. Do a natural release for 10 minutes. Serve topped with basil.

Korean-style Chicken

Servings: 6
Cooking Time: 35 Minutes

Ingredients:
- 3 green onions, sliced diagonally
- 3 chicken breasts, halved
- 5 tbsp sweet chili sauce
- 5 tbsp sriracha sauce
- 1 tbsp grated ginger
- 4 garlic cloves
- 1 tbsp rice vinegar
- 2 tbsp sesame seeds
- 1 tbsp soy sauce
- ½ cup chicken stock

Directions:
1. Combine chili sauce, sriracha sauce, ginger, garlic, vinegar, sesame seeds, soy sauce, and chicken stock in a bowl. Add in the chicken fillets and toss to coat. Transfer to your Instant Pot. Seal the lid, select Manual, and cook for 15 minutes on High pressure. Once ready, allow a natural release for 10 minutes and unlock the lid. Top with green onions and serve.

Hot Chicken With Garlic & Mushrooms

Servings: 4
Cooking Time: 30 Minutes

Ingredients:
- 1 cup button mushrooms, chopped
- 1 lb chicken breasts, cubed
- 2 cups chicken broth
- 2 tbsp flour
- 1 tsp cayenne pepper
- Salt and pepper to taste
- 2 tbsp olive oil
- 2 garlic cloves, chopped

Directions:
1. Warm the olive oil in your Instant Pot on Sauté. Add mushrooms, garlic, and chicken, season with salt, and stir-fry for 5 minutes, stirring occasionally until the veggies are tender. Pour in the chicken broth. Seal the lid. Cook on High Pressure for 8 minutes. Release the steam naturally for 10 minutes and stir in flour, cayenne, and black pepper. Cook for 5 minutes on Sauté. Serve warm.

Rigatoni With Turkey & Tomato Sauce

Servings: 4
Cooking Time: 30 Minutes

Ingredients:
- 2 tbsp canola oil
- 1 lb ground turkey
- 1 egg
- ¼ cup bread crumbs
- 2 cloves garlic, minced
- 1 tsp dried oregano
- 1 tsp cumin
- 1 tsp red pepper flakes
- Salt and pepper to taste
- 3 cups tomato sauce
- 8 oz rigatoni
- 2 tbsp grated Grana Padano

Directions:
1. In a bowl, combine turkey, crumbs, cumin, garlic, and egg. Season with oregano, salt, red pepper flakes, and pepper. Form the mixture into meatballs. Warm the oil on Sauté in your Instant Pot. Cook the meatballs for 3-4 minutes until browned on all sides; set aside.
2. Add rigatoni to the cooker and pour the tomato sauce over. Cover with water. Stir well. Throw in the meatballs. Seal the lid and cook for 4 minutes on High Pressure. Release the pressure quickly. Serve topped with cheese.

Chicken Gumbo

Servings: 4
Cooking Time: 40 Minutes

Ingredients:
- 4 chicken thighs
- 1 onion, diced
- 2 garlic cloves, minced
- 2 sticks celery, finely diced
- 2 green peppers, diced
- 1 tsp Cajun seasoning
- Salt and pepper to taste
- 2 tbsp olive oil
- 1 ½ cups tomato sauce
- 1 jalapeno, halved
- 2 tbsp sage, chopped

Directions:
1. Warm the olive oil in your Instant Pot on Sauté. Place in chicken and cook for 4-6 minutes on all sides; reserve. Add in onion, garlic, celery, and green peppers and cook for 5 minutes. Stir in Cajun seasoning, tomato sauce, salt, pepper, and 1 cup of water. Seal the lid, select Manual, and cook for

20 minutes on High pressure. When ready, perform a quick pressure release and unlock the lid. Top with sage and jalapeño pepper and serve.

Curried Chicken With Mushrooms

Servings: 4
Cooking Time: 25 Minutes

Ingredients:
- 1 cup shiitake mushrooms, sliced
- 1 cup white mushrooms, sliced
- 1 lb chicken breasts, cubed
- 2 tbsp olive oil
- 1 yellow onion, thinly sliced
- 1 tbsp curry paste
- 1 cup chicken stock
- ½ bunch cilantro, chopped

Directions:
1. Warm the olive oil in your Instant Pot on Sauté. Add in the chicken breasts and cook for 2 minutes until browned. Stir in onion and mushrooms and cook for another 3 minutes. Mix curry paste and chicken stock in a bowl and pour into the pot. Seal the lid, select Manual, and cook for 15 minutes on High pressure. Once ready, perform a quick pressure release and unlock the lid. Serve topped with cilantro.

Jamaican Chicken With Pineapple Sauce

Servings: 4
Cooking Time: 40 Minutes

Ingredients:
- 1 lb chicken thighs
- ½ cup coconut cream
- 2 tbsp soy sauce
- 1 cup pineapple chunks
- 1 tsp Jamaican seasoning
- 1 tsp coriander seeds
- ¼ tsp salt
- ½ cup cilantro, chopped
- 1 tsp arrowroot starch

Directions:
1. Place chicken thighs, coconut cream, soy sauce, Jamaican jerk seasoning, coriander seeds, and salt in your Instant Pot and stir. Pour in 1 cup of water and seal the lid; cook for 15 minutes on manual. Once over, allow a natural release for 10 minutes and unlock the lid.
2. Remove chicken to a bowl. Combine arrowroot starch

and 1 tbsp of water in a cup and pour it into the pot. Add in pineapple chunks and cook for 4-5 minutes on Sauté. Top the chicken with cilantro and sauce. Serve.

Turkey & Black Bean Chili

Servings: 6
Cooking Time: 30 Minutes

Ingredients:
- 2 lb chopped turkey breast
- 1 ½ cups vegetable stock
- 2 cans black beans
- 2 garlic cloves, peeled
- 1 onion, diced
- 1 yellow bell pepper, diced
- 1 green chiles, diced
- 1 can diced tomatoes
- 1 tbsp hot sauce
- ½ tsp cumin
- ½ tbsp chili powder
- 1 cup cheddar, shredded

Directions:
1. Place turkey, vegetable stock, black beans, garlic, onion, bell pepper, tomatoes, chiles, cumin, hot sauce, and chili powder in your Instant Pot and stir. Seal the lid, select Manual, and cook for 20 minutes on High pressure. Once done, allow a natural release for 10 minutes, then a quick pressure release, and unlock the lid. Top with cheddar and serve.

Caribbean Turkey Wings

Servings: 4
Cooking Time: 55 Minutes

Ingredients:
- 2 lb turkey wings
- 2 tbsp vegetable oil
- 2 tbsp butter
- Salt and pepper to taste
- 1 yellow onion, sliced
- ½ cup brown sugar
- 1 tbsp bonnet pepper sauce
- ¼ cup chives, chopped
- 1 cup pineapple juice
- 1 tbsp cornstarch

Directions:
1. Warm the vegetable oil and butter in your Instant Pot on Sauté. Sprinkle turkey wings with salt and pepper and place them in the pot. Sear for 5-6 minutes on all sides; set aside. Place onion in the pot and cook for 2 minutes. Stir in pineapple juice, bonnet pepper sauce, brown sugar, and 1/2 cup

of water. Put in turkey wings and seal the lid. Select Manual and cook for 20 minutes on High.
2. When done, allow a natural release for 10 minutes and unlock the lid. Remove wings to a plate. Mix cornstarch and some cooking liquid in a bowl and pour into the pot. Simmer for 5 minutes on Sauté until the sauce thickens. Top with chives and serve with sauce.

Bell Pepper & Chicken Stew

Servings: 4
Cooking Time: 30 Minutes

Ingredients:
- 1 lb chicken breasts, cubed
- 2 potatoes, peeled, chopped
- 5 bell peppers, chopped
- 2 carrots, chopped
- 2 ½ cups chicken broth
- 1 tomato, roughly chopped
- 2 tbsp chopped parsley
- 3 tbsp extra virgin olive oil
- 1 tsp cayenne pepper

Directions:
1. Warm the olive oil on Sauté in your Instant Pot. Stir-fry the bell peppers and carrots for 3 minutes. Add in the potatoes and tomato. Sprinkle with cayenne and stir well. Top with the chicken, pour in the broth, and seal the lid. Cook on High Pressure for 13 minutes. When ready, do a quick pressure release. Sprinkle with parsley and serve.

Weekend Turkey With Vegetables

Servings: 4
Cooking Time: 35 Minutes

Ingredients:
- 1 lb turkey breast, chopped
- 1 tsp red pepper flakes
- 2 cups canned tomatoes
- 3 cups chicken broth
- 1 tsp honey
- 2 cups zucchini, cubed
- 3 garlic cloves, chopped
- 1 onion, finely chopped
- 2 tbsp tomato paste
- 1 cup baby carrots, chopped
- Salt and pepper to taste
- 2 tbsp olive oil

Directions:
1. Mix turkey, red pepper flakes, tomatoes, broth, honey, zucchini, garlic, onion, tomato paste, carrots, salt, pepper,

and olive oil in your Instant Pot. Seal the lid and cook on Meat/Stew for 25 minutes on High Pressure. When ready, do a quick release and open the lid. Serve.

Quinoa Pilaf With Chicken

Servings: 4
Cooking Time: 35 Minutes

Ingredients:
- 1 lb chicken breasts, chopped
- 1 cup quinoa
- Salt and pepper to taste
- Greek yogurt for topping

Directions:
1. Add chicken and 2 cups of water to your Instant Pot. Seal the lid. Cook on Manual for 15 minutes on High. Do a quick release; remove the chicken. Add the quinoa to the pot and seal the lid again. Cook on Manual for 8 minutes on High. Do a quick release. Stir in the chicken and adjust the seasoning with salt and pepper. Plate and top with yogurt. Serve immediately.

Macaroni With Chicken & Pesto Sauce

Servings: 4
Cooking Time: 20 Minutes

Ingredients:
- 3 ½ cups water
- 4 chicken breasts, cubed
- 8 oz macaroni pasta
- 1 tbsp butter
- Salt and pepper to taste
- 1 lb collard greens, trimmed
- 1 cup cherry tomatoes, halved
- ½ cup basil pesto sauce
- ¼ cup cream cheese
- 1 garlic clove, minced
- ¼ cup asiago cheese, grated
- 2 tbsp chopped basil

Directions:
1. Mix water, chicken, salt, butter, and macaroni in the Instant Pot. Seal the lid and cook for 2 minutes on High Pressure. Release the pressure quickly. Carefully open the lid, get rid of ¼ cup water from the pot. Set to Sauté.
2. Into the pot, mix in collard greens, pesto sauce, garlic, salt, cream cheese, cherry tomatoes, and black pepper. Cook for 1-2 minutes as you stir until sauce is creamy. Place the pasta into serving plates. Top with asiago cheese and basil

before serving.

Garlic Chicken

Servings: 4
Cooking Time: 35 Minutes

Ingredients:
- 1 lb chicken breasts
- Salt and pepper to taste
- 2 tbsp butter
- 1 cup chicken broth
- 2 garlic cloves, minced
- 2 tbsp tarragon, chopped

Directions:
1. Place chicken breasts in your Instant Pot. Sprinkle with garlic, salt, and pepper. Pour in the chicken broth and butter. Seal the lid, select Manual, and cook for 15 minutes on High pressure.
2. When over, allow a natural release for 10 minutes and unlock the lid. Remove the chicken and shred it. Top with tarragon and serve.

Easy Chicken With Capers & Tomatoes

Servings: 4
Cooking Time: 35 Minutes

Ingredients:
- 4 chicken legs
- Salt and pepper to taste
- 2 tbsp olive oil
- 1 onion, diced
- 2 garlic cloves, minced
- 1/3 cup red wine
- 2 cups diced tomatoes
- 1/3 cup capers
- 2 pickles, chopped

Directions:
1. Sprinkle pepper and salt over the chicken. Warm oil on Sauté in your Instant Pot. Add in onion and Sauté for 3 minutes until fragrant. Add in garlic and cook for 30 seconds. Mix the chicken with vegetables and cook for 6 to 7 minutes until lightly browned.
2. Add the red wine to the pan to deglaze, scraping the pan's bottom to eliminate any browned bits of food. Stir in tomatoes. Seal the lid and cook on High Pressure for 12 minutes. Release the pressure quickly. To the chicken mixture, add the capers and pickles. Serve the chicken topped with the tomato sauce and enjoy!

Sweet & Citrusy Chicken Breasts

Servings: 4
Cooking Time: 20 Minutes

Ingredients:
- 2 chicken breasts, cubed
- ½ cup honey
- ½ cup orange juice
- 1/3 cup soy sauce
- 1/3 cup chicken stock
- 1/3 cup hoisin sauce
- 1 garlic clove, minced
- 2 tsp cornstarch
- 2 tsp water
- 1 cup diced orange
- 3 cups cooked quinoa

Directions:
1. Arrange the chicken at the bottom of your Instant Pot. In a bowl, stir honey, soy sauce, garlic, hoisin sauce, stock, and orange juice until the honey is dissolved. Pour the mixture over the chicken. Seal the lid and cook on High Pressure for 7 minutes. Release the pressure quickly.
2. Take the chicken from the pot and set it in a bowl. Press Sauté. In a small bowl, mix water with cornstarch. Pour into the liquid within the pot and cook for 3 minutes until thick. Stir diced orange and chicken into the sauce until well coated. Serve with quinoa.

Honey-glazed Turkey

Servings: 4
Cooking Time: 60 Minutes

Ingredients:
- 1 large turkey breast
- ½ cup honey
- ½ tsp cumin
- ½ tsp turmeric
- Salt and pepper to taste
- 2 cups chicken stock
- 1 onion, diced
- 2 garlic cloves, minced
- 1 tbsp dry sherry

Directions:
1. Combine honey, cumin, turmeric, salt, and pepper in a bowl. Rub the mixture onto the turkey and let sit for 10 minutes. Place onion, garlic, and turkey in your Instant Pot. Add in chicken stock and sherry. Seal the lid and cook for 30 minutes on Manual. When ready, allow a natural release for 10 minutes. Slice turkey before serving.

Turkey Cakes With Ginger Gravy

Servings: 4
Cooking Time: 25 Minutes

Ingredients:
- 1 lb ground turkey
- ¼ cup breadcrumbs
- ¼ cup grated Parmesan
- ½ tsp garlic powder
- 2 green onions, chopped
- Salt and pepper to taste
- 2 tbsp olive oil
- 2 cups tomatoes, diced
- ¼ cup chicken broth
- Ginger sauce
- 4 tbsp soy sauce
- 2 tbsp canola oil
- 2 tbsp rice vinegar
- 1 garlic clove, minced
- 1 tsp ginger, grated
- ½ tbsp honey
- ¼ tsp black pepper
- ½ tbsp cornstarch

Directions:
1. Combine turkey, breadcrumbs, green onions, garlic powder, salt, pepper, and Parmesan cheese in a bowl. Mix with your hands and shape meatballs out of the mixture. In another bowl, mix soy sauce, canola oil, rice vinegar, garlic clove, ginger, honey, pepper, and cornstarch. Warm the olive oil in your Instant Pot on Sauté.
2. Place in meatballs and cook for 4 minutes on all sides. Pour in ginger gravy, tomatoes, and chicken stock and seal the lid. Select Manual and cook for 10 minutes on High pressure. Once over, perform a quick pressure release and unlock the lid. Serve in individual bowls.

Spicy Honey Chicken

Servings: 4
Cooking Time: 20 Minutes

Ingredients:
- 4 chicken drumsticks
- 5 tbsp soy sauce
- 2 tbsp honey
- 1 cup chicken broth
- 1 garlic clove, minced
- 2 tbsp hot chili sauce
- 2 tbsp cornstarch
- 1 lime, cut into wedges

Directions:
1. Place soy sauce, honey, garlic, and chili sauce in your Instant Pot and stir. Add in chicken drumsticks and toss to coat. Pour in chicken broth and seal the lid. Select Manual and cook for 12 minutes on High pressure. Mix 2 tbsp of water and cornstarch in a bowl.
2. When over, perform a quick pressure release and unlock the lid. Add in the slurry and simmer on Sauté until the sauce thickens. Serve right away with lime wedges.

Sticky Chicken Wings

Servings: 6
Cooking Time: 35 Minutes + Marinating Time

Ingredients:
- 2 lb chicken wings
- 3 tbsp light brown sugar
- 2 tbsp soy sauce
- 1 small lime, juiced
- ½ tsp sea salt
- 1 tsp five-spice powder

Directions:
1. Combine soy sauce, lime juice, five-spice powder, brown sugar, and salt in a bowl. Place chicken wing and marinade in a resealable bag and shake it. Transfer to the fridge and let marinate for 30 minutes.
2. Pour 1/2 cup of water and marinate chicken wings with the juices in your Instant Pot. Seal the lid, select Manual, and cook for 15 minutes on High pressure. When done, allow a natural release for 10 minutes and unlock the lid. Cook on Sauté until the sauce thickens. Serve.

Chimichurri Chicken

Servings: 6
Cooking Time: 25 Minutes

Ingredients:
- 2 lb chicken breasts
- 1 cup chicken broth
- 1 tsp smoked paprika
- 1 tsp cumin
- Salt and pepper to taste
- 2 cups chimichurri salsa

Directions:
1. Sprinkle chicken breasts with paprika, cumin, salt, and pepper. Place the chicken broth with chicken breasts in your Instant Pot. Seal the lid, select Manual, and cook for 15 minutes on High pressure. Once done, perform a quick pressure release and unlock the lid. Cut the chicken into slices and top with chimichurri sauce. Serve.

Best Italian Chicken Balls

Servings: 4
Cooking Time: 35 Minutes

Ingredients:
- 1/3 cup blue cheese, crumbled
- ¼ cup Pecorino Romano cheese, shredded
- 1 lb ground chicken
- 3 tbsp red hot sauce
- 1 egg
- ¼ cup breadcrumbs
- 1 tbsp ranch dressing
- 1 tbsp fresh basil, chopped
- Salt and pepper to taste
- 15 oz canned tomato sauce
- 1 cup chicken broth
- 2 tbsp olive oil

Directions:
1. In a bowl, mix ground chicken, egg, Pecorino cheese, pepper, salt, ranch dressing, blue cheese, hot sauce, and breadcrumbs. Shape the mixture into balls. Warm oil on Sauté in your Instant Pot. Add in the meatballs and cook for 2-3 minutes until browned on all sides.
2. Add in tomato sauce and broth. Seal the lid and cook on High Pressure for 7 minutes. Release the pressure quickly. Remove meatballs carefully and place them on a serving plate. Top with basil and serve.

Awesome Chicken In Tikka Masala Sauce

Servings: 4
Cooking Time: 30 Minutes

Ingredients:
- 2 lb boneless, skinless chicken thighs
- Salt and pepper to taste
- 1 ½ tbsp olive oil
- ½ onion, chopped
- 2 garlic cloves, minced
- 3 tbsp tomato puree
- 1 tsp fresh ginger, minced
- 1 tbsp garam masala
- 2 tsp curry powder
- 1 tsp ground coriander
- ½ tsp ground cumin
- 1 jalapeño pepper, minced
- 29 oz canned tomato sauce
- 3 tomatoes, chopped
- ½ cup natural yogurt
- 1 lemon, juiced
- ¼ cup chopped cilantro
- 4 lemon wedges

Directions:
1. Rub black pepper and salt onto the chicken. Warm oil on Sauté in your Instant Pot. Add garlic and onion and cook for 3 minutes until soft. Stir in tomato puree, garam masala, cumin, curry powder, ginger, coriander, and jalapeño pepper; cook for 30 seconds until fragrant.
2. Stir in tomato sauce and tomatoes. Simmer the mixture as you scrape the bottom to get rid of any browned bits. Stir in chicken to coat. Seal the lid and cook on High Pressure for 10 minutes. Release the pressure quickly.
3. Press Sauté and simmer the sauce and cook for 5 minutes until thickened. Stir lemon juice and yogurt through the sauce. Serve garnished with lemon wedges and cilantro.

Turkey Stew With Salsa Verde

Servings: 4
Cooking Time: 52 Minutes

Ingredients:
- 1 lb turkey thighs, boneless and diced
- 2 tbsp olive oil
- 1 cup pearl onions
- 1 carrot, julienned
- 1 cup green peas
- 1 cup salsa verde
- Salt and pepper to taste
- ¼ tsp turmeric
- ¼ tsp cumin

Directions:
1. Warm olive oil in your IP on Sauté. Add in the turkey pieces and brown for 4-5 minutes, stirring occasionally; set aside. Add pearl onions and carrot to the pot and sauté for 3-4 minutes. Stir in the turmeric, cumin, salt, and pepper and pour in 1 cup of water. Return the turkey.
2. Seal the lid, select Manual, and cook for 20 minutes on High. Once ready, allow a natural pressure release for 10 minutes. Unlock the lid, add in the green peas and salsa verde, and stir. Press Sauté and cook for 3 minutes.

Chapter 5 Pork, Beef & Lamb

Chapter 5 Pork, Beef & Lamb

Classic Beef Stroganoff

Servings: 6
Cooking Time: 45 Minutes

Ingredients:
- 2 lb chuck roast, thin slices
- 2 tbsp butter
- 1 tbsp olive oil
- 1 onion, sliced
- Salt and pepper to taste
- 1 cup mushrooms, sliced
- 2 garlic cloves, minced
- 1 ¼ cups beef broth
- ½ cup crème fraiche
- 2 cup cooked rice

Directions:
1. Warm the olive oil and butter in your Instant Pot on Sauté. Place in onion and cook for 3 minutes. Sprinkle chuck roast with salt and pepper and place it in the pot and brown for 2 minutes on all sides. Add in mushrooms and garlic and cook for another 3 minutes. Stir in beef broth and seal the lid.
2. Select Manual and cook for 20 minutes on High pressure. Once ready, perform a quick pressure release and unlock the lid. Mix in créme fraiche and lock the lid. Let sit for 5 minutes. Serve with rice.

Easy Wax Beans With Ground Beef

Servings: 4
Cooking Time: 20 Minutes

Ingredients:
- 1 lb ground beef
- 1 lb wax beans
- 1 small onion, chopped
- 1 tbsp tomato paste
- 2 cups beef broth
- 2 garlic cloves, crushed
- 2 tbsp olive oil
- 2 tbsp parsley, chopped
- 1 tsp salt
- ½ tsp paprika
- 1 tbsp Parmesan, grated

Directions:
1. Grease the pot with olive oil. Stir-fry the onion and garlic for a few minutes until translucent on Sauté. Add beef, tomato paste, parsley, salt, and paprika. Cook for 5 more minutes, stirring constantly. Add wax beans and beef broth. Press Cancel and seal the lid. Cook on High Pressure for 4 minutes. Do a natural release. Carefully unlock the lid. Top with Parmesan and serve hot.

Pork Chops With Creamy Gravy & Broccoli

Servings: 6
Cooking Time: 35 Minutes

Ingredients:
- Pork Chops
- Salt and pepper to taste
- 1 tsp garlic powder
- 1 tsp onion powder
- 1 tsp red pepper flakes
- 6 boneless pork chops
- 10 broccoli florets
- 1 cup vegetable stock
- ¼ cup butter, melted
- ¼ cup milk
- Gravy
- 3 tbsp flour
- ½ cup heavy cream
- Salt and pepper to taste

Directions:
1. Combine salt, garlic powder, pepper flakes, onion, and pepper. Rub the mixture onto pork chops. Place stock, milk, and broccoli in the Instant Pot. Lay the pork chops on top. Seal the lid and cook for 15 minutes on High Pressure. Release the pressure quickly.
2. Transfer the pork chops and broccoli to a plate. Press Sauté and simmer the liquid remaining in the pot. Mix cream and flour. Pour into the simmering liquid and cook

for 4 to 6 minutes until thickened and bubbly. Season with pepper and salt. Top the chops with gravy, drizzle butter over broccoli, and serve.

Short Ribs With Wine Mushroom Sauce

Servings: 4
Cooking Time: 75 Minutes

Ingredients:
- 2 lb boneless pork short ribs, cut into 3-inch pieces
- Salt and pepper to taste
- ½ onion, chopped
- ½ cup red wine
- 3 tbsp olive oil
- ½ tbsp tomato paste
- 2 carrots, sliced
- 2 cups mushrooms, sliced
- 1 tbsp cornstarch
- Minced parsley to garnish

Directions:
1. Rub the ribs on all sides with salt and pepper. Heat the oil on Sauté in your Instant Pot and brown short ribs on all sides, about 6-7 minutes. Remove to a plate. Add onion to the pot and cook for 3-5 minutes. Pour in wine and tomato paste to deglaze by scraping any browned bits from the bottom of the cooker. Cook for 2 minutes until the wine has reduced slightly. Return ribs to the pot and cover with carrots. Pour 1 cup of water over.
2. Seal the lid, and select Manual on High Pressure for 35 minutes. When ready, let the pressure release naturally for 10 minutes. Carefully unlock the lid. Transfer ribs and carrots to a plate. To the pot, add mushrooms. Press Sauté and cook them for 2-4 minutes. In a bowl, add 2 tbsp of water and cornstarch and mix until smooth. Pour this slurry into the pot, stirring constantly until it thickens slightly, 2 minutes. Season the gravy with salt and pepper. Pour over the ribs and garnish with parsley.

Delicious Pork In Button Mushroom Gravy

Servings: 6
Cooking Time: 60 Minutes

Ingredients:
- 1 cup button mushrooms, chopped
- Salt and garlic powder to taste
- 2 lb pork shoulder
- 2 tbsp butter, unsalted
- 1 tbsp balsamic vinegar
- ¼ cup soy sauce
- 2 bay leaves
- 1 cup beef broth
- 2 tbsp cornstarch

Directions:
1. Rub the pork with salt and garlic powder. Melt butter on Sauté. Brown the meat for 5 minutes on each side. Stir in soy sauce and bay leaves. Cook for 2 minutes. Add in beef broth and balsamic vinegar. Seal the lid and set to Meat/Stew. Cook for 30 minutes on High Pressure.
2. When done, do a quick release. Remove and discard the bay leaves. Stir in mushrooms. Cook for about 8 minutes on Sauté. Stir in cornstarch and cook for 2 minutes.

Lamb Chorba

Servings: 4
Cooking Time: 35 Minutes

Ingredients:
- 2 lb lamb shanks
- 2 tbsp olive oil
- 2 garlic cloves, peeled
- 1 onion, chopped
- 1 celery stalk, chopped
- 1 tomato, chopped
- 1 carrot, chopped
- 2 tbsp oregano, chopped
- Salt and pepper to taste
- 4 cups vegetable broth
- 1 tbsp white wine vinegar

Directions:
1. Warm the olive oil in your Instant Pot on Sauté. Place in the lamb, celery, onion, carrot, and garlic and sauté for 6 minutes. Stir in vegetable broth, tomato, salt, and pepper. Seal the lid. Select Manual and cook for 20 minutes. Release the pressure quickly. Drizzle with vinegar and sprinkle with oregano to serve.

Beef Tikka Masala

Servings: 4
Cooking Time: 50 Minutes

Ingredients:
- 2 tbsp tikka masala powder
- 1 lb beef chuck steak, cubed
- 2 tbsp olive oil
- 1 green chili, chopped
- 2 tsp ginger purée
- 2 tsp garlic purée
- 1 onion, chopped
- 1 cup beef broth
- 1 diced tomatoes
- ½ cup coconut cream
- Salt and pepper to taste
- 3 tbsp chopped cilantro

Directions:
1. Warm the olive oil in your Instant Pot on Sauté. Sprinkle beef steak with salt and pepper. Place it in the pot and sauté for 4-5 minutes, stirring periodically; set aside. Add onion, ginger puree, garlic puree, green chili, tikka masala powder, salt, and pepper in the pot.
2. Cook for 3 minutes. Pour in beef broth and scrape any brown bits from the bottom. Put back beef to the pot and diced tomatoes and seal the lid. Select Manual and cook for 25 minutes on High pressure.
3. Once done, perform a quick pressure release and unlock the lid. Mix in coconut cream for 4-5 minutes. Scatter cilantro on top and serve.

Best Pork Chops With Bbq Sauce & Veggies

Servings: 4
Cooking Time: 25 Minutes

Ingredients:
- 4 pork rib chops
- 1 cup carrots, thinly sliced
- 1 cup turnips, thinly sliced
- 1 cup onions, slice into rings
- 1 ½ cups BBQ sauce
- 2 cups water

Directions:
1. Add the pork chops to your cooker. Pour in ½ cup of BBQ sauce and 2 cups of water. Select Meat/Stew. Stir in the onions, turnips, and carrots. Lock the lid and cook for 20 minutes on High. Once ready, Release the pressure quickly. Open the lid, drizzle with the remaining BBQ

sauce and serve warm.

Melt-in-your-mouth Meatballs

Servings:4
Cooking Time: 16 Minutes

Ingredients:
- 1 pound 80/20 ground beef
- ¼ cup grated Parmesan cheese
- 1 large egg, lightly beaten
- 1 tablespoon Italian seasoning
- 1 cup panko bread crumbs
- ½ teaspoon garlic salt
- ½ teaspoon ground black pepper
- 2 tablespoons olive oil
- 1 cup marinara sauce
- 2 cups water

Directions:
1. In a medium bowl, combine beef, cheese, egg, Italian seasoning, bread crumbs, garlic salt, and pepper. If stiff, add 1–2 tablespoons water. Form mixture into eight meatballs. Set aside.
2. Press the Sauté button on the Instant Pot and heat oil. Place meatballs around the edge of pot. Sear all sides of meatballs, about 4 minutes total. Press the Cancel button.
3. Transfer seared meatballs to a 7-cup glass baking dish. Top with marinara sauce. Discard extra juice and oil from pot.
4. Add water to the Instant Pot and insert steam rack. Place glass baking dish on top of steam rack. Lock lid.
5. Press the Manual or Pressure Cook button and adjust time to 12 minutes. When timer beeps, let pressure release naturally for 10 minutes. Quick-release any additional pressure until float valve drops. Unlock lid.
6. Transfer meatballs to plates. Serve warm.

Traditional Lamb With Vegetables

Servings: 6
Cooking Time: 30 Minutes

Ingredients:
- 1 lb lamb chops, 1-inch thick
- 1 cup green peas, rinsed
- 3 carrots, chopped
- 3 onions, chopped
- 1 potato, chopped
- 1 tomato, chopped
- 3 tbsp olive oil
- 1 tbsp paprika
- Salt and pepper to taste

Directions:

1. Grease the Instant Pot with olive oil. Rub salt onto the lamb and make a bottom layer. Add peas, carrots, onions, potato, and tomato. Season with paprika. Add olive oil, 1 cup of water, salt, and pepper. Give it a good stir and seal the lid. Cook on Meat/Stew for 20 minutes on High Pressure. When ready, do a natural pressure release. Carefully unlock the lid. Serve hot.

Easy Pork Fillets With Peachy Sauce

Servings: 6
Cooking Time: 30 Minutes

Ingredients:
- 1 lb pork loin fillets
- 16 oz canned peach
- ½ tsp ground coriander
- ½ tsp ginger, chopped
- ½ cup Worcestershire sauce
- ¼ cup apple cider vinegar
- ½ tsp garlic, minced
- Salt and pepper to taste
- 1 cup onions, sliced
- 2 tbsp olive oil
- 1 cup tomato sauce
- 1 tbsp arrowroot slurry

Directions:

1. On Sauté, heat oil. Cook onions until tender, about 4 minutes. Stir in pork, peaches, coriander, ginger, Worcestershire sauce, apple vinegar, garlic, salt, pepper, and tomato sauce. Seal the lid, Select Meat/Stew, and cook for 20 minutes. Do a quick pressure release. Stir in the slurry and cook on Sauté until the sauce thickens.

Pulled Pork

Servings: 8
Cooking Time: 70 Minutes

Ingredients:
- ½ boneless pork shoulder, quartered
- 2 teaspoons salt
- 1 teaspoon ground black pepper
- 2 tablespoons olive oil
- 2 cups beef broth

Directions:

1. Season all sides of pork with salt and pepper.
2. Press the Sauté button on the Instant Pot and heat oil. Place pork in pot. Sear meat for 5 minutes, making sure to get each side.
3. Add broth to pot. Press the Cancel button. Lock lid.

4. Press the Manual or Pressure Cook button and adjust time to 65 minutes. When timer beeps, let pressure release naturally for 10 minutes. Quick-release any additional pressure until float valve drops. Unlock lid.
5. Remove a few ladles of liquid from pot, as most is just fat rendered from pork.
6. Using two forks, shred pork and incorporate juices. Remove any additional unwanted liquid. Serve warm.

Leftover Beef Sandwiches

Servings: 4
Cooking Time: 30 Minutes

Ingredients:
- 1 lb leftover roast beef
- 4 ciabatta rolls
- Salt and pepper to taste
- 1 tsp brown sugar
- ½ tsp garlic powder
- 1 tsp mustard powder
- 1 tsp paprika
- 2 tsp onion flakes
- 2 cups beef stock
- 2 tbsp Worcestershire sauce
- 1 tbsp balsamic vinegar
- 4 tsp butter, softened
- 4 cheddar cheese slices

Directions:

1. In a bowl, mix salt, pepper, sugar, garlic powder, mustard powder, paprika, and onion flakes and rub the beef roast with the mixture. Transfer to your Instant Pot and add beef stock, Worcestershire sauce, and balsamic vinegar.
2. Seal the lid, select Manual, and cook for 10 minutes on High pressure. When over, allow a natural release for 10 minutes, then perform a quick pressure release, and unlock the lid. Remove beef roast and shred it.
3. Discard sauce and reserve 1 cup for serving. Brush ciabatta rolls with butter and top with cheddar cheese. Stuff the rolls with some shredded beef. Serve sandwiches with sauce.

Maple Pork Carnitas

Servings: 6
Cooking Time: 50 Minutes

Ingredients:
- 10 sundried tomatoes, diced
- 2 lb pork butt roast
- ¼ cup maple syrup
- 2 cups beef stock
- 1 tbsp mustard powder
- 1 tsp onion powder
- Salt to taste
- 3 tbsp cilantro, chopped
- 1 jalapeno, chopped
- 6 warm tortillas

Directions:
1. Rub the meat with salt, mustard powder, and onion powder and place it in the Instant Pot. Mix the stock and maple syrup in bowl; stir in the tomatoes and jalapeño. Pour the mixture over the pork. Seal the lid and cook on High Pressure for 30 minutes. Allow the pressure to release naturally for 10 minutes. Shred the pork with two forks. Add it to the tortillas. Top with cilantro to serve.

Quick French-style Lamb With Sesame

Servings: 4
Cooking Time: 45 Minutes

Ingredients:
- 12 oz lamb, tender cuts, ½-inch thick
- 1 cup rice
- 1 cup green peas
- 3 tbsp sesame seeds
- 4 cups beef broth
- 1 tsp salt
- ½ tsp dried thyme
- 3 tbsp butter

Directions:
1. Mix the meat in the pot with broth. Seal the lid and cook on High Pressure for 15 minutes. Do a quick release. Remove the meat but keep the liquid. Add rice and green peas. Season with salt and thyme. Stir well and top with the meat. Seal the lid and cook on Manual for 18 minutes on High. Do a quick release. Carefully unlock the lid. Stir in butter and sesame seeds. Serve immediately.

Cilantro Pork With Avocado

Servings: 4
Cooking Time: 45 Minutes + Marinating Time

Ingredients:
- 1 lb pork tenderloin, cut into strips
- 3 garlic cloves, chopped
- ½ tsp oregano
- ½ tsp ground cumin
- 1 tbsp Hungarian paprika
- 2 tbsp olive oil
- 2 cups chicken stock
- Salt and pepper to taste
- 1 avocado, sliced
- 2 tbsp cilantro, chopped

Directions:
1. Mix garlic, oregano, cumin, paprika, salt, and pepper in a bowl. Add in pork strips and toss to coat. Let marinate for 30 minutes in the fridge. Warm the olive oil in your Instant Pot on Sauté. Place the strips in the pot and sauté for 10 minutes. Stir in chicken stock and seal the lid. Select Manual and cook for 15 minutes on High pressure.
2. When done, allow a natural release for 10 minutes, then perform a quick pressure release, and unlock the lid. Scatter with cilantro. Serve topped with avocado slices.

Pear & Cider Pork Tenderloin

Servings: 4
Cooking Time: 55 Minutes

Ingredients:
- 1 lb pork loin
- 1 tbsp garlic powder
- 2 tbsp olive oil
- 1 yellow onion, chopped
- 2 pears, cored and chopped
- 1 cup apple cider
- 1 tbsp fennel seeds
- Salt and pepper to taste

Directions:
1. Sprinkle pork loin with salt, pepper, and garlic powder. Warm the olive oil in your Instant Pot on Sauté. Place the loin and sear for 8 minutes on all sides. Set aside. Add onion to the pot and cook for 3 minutes. Put in pears and apple cider and scrape any brown bits from the bottom. Put loin back to the pot along with fennel seeds.
2. Seal the lid. Select Manual and cook for 20 minutes on High pressure. When ready, allow a natural release for 10 minutes and unlock the lid. Slice the pork loin before serving and top with sauce.

Pork With Onions & Cream Sauce

Servings: 6
Cooking Time: 52 Minutes

Ingredients:
- 1 ½ lb pork shoulder, cut into pieces
- 2 onions, chopped
- 1 ½ cups sour cream
- 1 cup tomato puree
- ½ tbsp cilantro
- ¼ tsp cumin
- ¼ tsp cayenne pepper
- 1 garlic clove, minced
- Salt and pepper to taste

Directions:
1. Coat with cooking spray the inner pot and add the pork. Cook for 3-4 minutes on Sauté until lightly browned. Add onions and garlic and cook for 3 minutes until fragrant. Press Cancel. Stir in sour cream, tomato puree, cilantro, cumin, cayenne pepper, salt, and pepper and seal the lid. Select Soup/Broth and cook for 30 minutes on High. Let sit for 5 minutes before quickly release the pressure.

Tasty Beef Cutlets With Vegetables

Servings: 4
Cooking Time: 45 Minutes

Ingredients:
- 2 large beef cutlets
- 4 whole potatoes, peeled
- 1 whole onion, peeled
- 1 whole carrot, peeled
- 10 oz cauliflower florets
- 3 tbsp olive oil
- 1 tbsp butter
- Salt and pepper to taste
- 3 cups beef broth

Directions:
1. Sprinkle the meat with salt and pepper and place it in your Instant Pot. Add in cauliflower, onion, carrot, and potatoes. Pour in broth, seal the lid, and cook on High Pressure for 25 minutes. Release the pressure naturally for about 10 minutes. Remove the meat and vegetables. Melt butter and oil on Sauté. Add the meat. Brown on both sides and serve with vegetables.

Gruyere Mushroom & Mortadella Cups

Servings: 4
Cooking Time: 20 Minutes

Ingredients:
- 4 eggs, beaten
- 1 tsp olive oil
- ½ tsp paprika
- ½ cup mushrooms, chopped
- 1 cup mortadella, chopped
- 1 tbsp parsley, minced
- Salt and pepper to taste
- 2 tbsp Gruyere, grated

Directions:
1. Mix the eggs, olive oil, 1 tbsp of water, and paprika in a bowl. Add in mushrooms, parsley, salt, pepper, and mortadella. Divide the mixture between ramekins and top with Gruyere cheese.
2. Pour 1 cup of water into your Instant Pot and fit in a trivet. Place the ramekins on the trivet and seal the lid. Select Manual and cook for 12 minutes on High pressure. Once ready, perform a quick pressure release. Carefully unlock the lid. Serve warm.

Quick And Easy Meatloaf

Servings: 6
Cooking Time: 35 Minutes

Ingredients:
- 1 pound ground beef
- 1 pound ground pork
- 4 large eggs
- 1 cup panko bread crumbs
- 1 large shallot, finely diced
- ¼ cup seeded and finely diced red bell pepper
- ½ cup tomato sauce
- 1 tablespoon Italian seasoning
- ½ teaspoon smoked paprika
- ½ teaspoon garlic powder
- ½ teaspoon celery seed
- 1 teaspoon sea salt
- ½ teaspoon ground black pepper
- 1 cup beef broth

Directions:
1. Using your hands, in a large bowl combine all ingredients except the broth.
2. Form mixture into a ball, flatten the top, then place meatloaf into a 7-cup glass dish.

3. Add beef broth to the Instant Pot. Insert trivet. Place glass dish on top of the trivet. Lock lid.

4. Press the Meat button and cook for the default time of 35 minutes. When timer beeps, let pressure release naturally for 10 minutes. Quick-release any additional pressure until float valve drops and then unlock lid.

5. Remove meatloaf from Instant Pot and let cool at room temperature for 10 minutes. Tilt glass bowl over the sink and pour out any liquid/rendered fat. Slice and serve.

Bbq Pork Lettuce Cups

Servings: 6
Cooking Time: 60 Minutes

Ingredients:
- 1-2 little gem lettuces, leaves separated
- 3 lb pork roast, cut into chunks
- 2 tbsp olive oil
- Salt and pepper to taste
- 1 cup chicken broth
- ½ cup BBQ sauce
- 1 red onion, thinly sliced
- 2 tbsp cilantro, chopped

Directions:
1. Sprinkle pork roast with salt and pepper. Place the roast, olive oil, chicken broth, and BBQ sauce in your Instant Pot and stir. Seal the lid, select Manual, and cook for 40 minutes on High. When ready, allow a natural release for 10 minutes, then perform a quick pressure release, and unlock the lid. Remove roast and shred it using two forks. Divide shredded pork between lettuce leaves. Scatter with onion and cilantro. Serve with the gravy.

Easy Lamb & Spinach Soup

Servings: 5
Cooking Time: 45 Minutes

Ingredients:
- 1 lb lamb shoulder, cubed
- 10 oz spinach, chopped
- 3 eggs, beaten
- 5 cups vegetable broth
- 3 tbsp olive oil
- 1 tsp salt

Directions:
1. Place in your Instant Pot the lamb, spinach, eggs, broth, olive oil, and salt. Seal the lid, press Soup/Broth, and cook for 30 minutes on High Pressure. Do a natural pressure release for about 10 minutes. Serve warm.

Wine Pork Butt With Fennel & Mushrooms

Servings: 4
Cooking Time: 30 Minutes

Ingredients:
- 3 tbsp olive oil
- 1 lb pork butt, sliced
- 2 cups mushrooms, sliced
- 1 fennel bulb, chopped
- ½ cup white wine
- 1 tsp garlic, minced
- ½ cup vegetable broth

Directions:
1. Heat the olive oil on Sauté. Brown the pork slices and for a few minutes. Stir in mushrooms, fennel, wine, garlic, and broth. Seal the lid and cook for 20 minutes on Manual on High. When done, do a quick release. Serve.

Hot Paprika & Oregano Lamb

Servings: 4
Cooking Time: 70 Minutes + Marinating Time

Ingredients:
- 1 lb lamb shoulder
- 1 tsp hot paprika
- 1 tsp oregano
- 1 tsp cumin
- ¼ tsp ground cinnamon
- 2 tbsp tomato puree
- ¼ cup red wine
- ¼ cup chicken stock
- 1 tbsp olive oil
- ½ cup water
- 2 tbsp butter
- Salt and pepper to taste

Directions:
1. Mix the oregano, hot paprika, salt, black pepper, cumin, and cinnamon in a bowl. Add in lamb and toss to coat. Cover and let marinate for 20-30 minutes. Warm the olive oil in your Instant Pot on Sauté. Place in lamb shoulder and brown for 5 minutes on all sides. Pour in red wine, chicken stock, tomato puree, butter, and ½ cup of water.

2. Seal the lid, select Manual, and cook for 45 minutes on High pressure. Once over, allow a natural release for 10 minutes, then perform a quick pressure release, and unlock the lid. Remove the lamb to a cutting board shred it. Return to the pot and stir. Serve warm.

Chipotle Shredded Beef

Servings: 4
Cooking Time: 45 Minutes

Ingredients:
- 2 lb beef shoulder roast
- 2 tbsp vegetable oil
- 1 onion, chopped
- 3 garlic cloves, minced
- 3 cups beef broth
- 2 tbsp tomato salsa
- 1 tsp chipotle chili pepper
- Salt and pepper to taste
- 4 tbsp sour cream
- 2 tbsp cilantro, chopped

Directions:
1. Rub the beef roast with chipotle chili pepper, salt, and pepper on all sides. Warm the vegetable oil in your Instant Pot on Sauté. Place the onion and garlic and cook for 2-3 minutes. Add in the beef roast and beef broth and seal the lid.
2. Select Manual and cook for 30 minutes on High pressure. Once ready, perform a quick pressure release and unlock the lid. Remove meat and shred it. Pour tomato salsa in the pot and cook until the sauce thickens on Sauté. Stir in shredded beef. Top with cilantro and serve with a dollop of sour cream on the side.

Beef Meatballs With Tomato-basil Sauce

Servings: 4
Cooking Time: 30 Minutes

Ingredients:
- 2 cups tomato and basil pasta sauce
- 1 ¼ lb ground beef
- 1 tsp garlic powder
- 1 tsp onion powder
- 1 tsp oregano
- 2 tbsp breadcrumbs
- Salt and pepper to taste
- 2 tbsp olive oil

Directions:
1. Combine ground beef, garlic powder, onion powder, oregano, breadcrumbs, salt, and pepper in a bowl. Make 2-inch meatballs of the mixture. Warm the olive oil in your Instant Pot on Sauté. Add in the meatballs and cook for 4-5 minutes on all sides until browned. Stir in tomato and basil pasta sauce and ¼ cup of water.

2. Seal the lid, select Manual, and cook for 10 minutes on High pressure. When done, allow a natural release for 10 minutes, then perform a quick pressure release, and unlock the lid. Serve immediately.

Beef Neapolitan Ragù

Servings: 4
Cooking Time: 53 Minutes

Ingredients:
- 1 ½ lb beef steak, cut into strips
- 2 tbsp lard
- 1 onion, chopped
- 2 cups crushed tomatoes
- 1 carrot, chopped
- 1 celery stalk, chopped
- 1 cup beef broth
- ½ cup red wine
- 1 tbsp passata
- Salt and pepper to taste

Directions:
1. Melt lard in your Instant Pot on Sauté. Place in onion, carrot, and celery and sauté until fragrant. Add in beef steak and cook for 3 minutes, stirring often. Pour in tomatoes, beef broth, red wine, passata, salt, and pepper and seal the lid. Select Meat/Stew.
2. Cook for 30 minutes on High pressure. When over, allow a natural release for 10 minutes, then perform a quick pressure release, and unlock the lid. Serve immediately.

Chapter 6 Fish & Seafood

Seafood Chowder With Oyster Crackers

Servings: 4
Cooking Time: 40 Minutes

Ingredients:
- 20 oz canned mussels, drained, liquid reserved
- ¼ cup grated Pecorino Romano cheese
- 1 lb potatoes, peeled and cut chunks
- 2 cups oyster crackers
- 2 tbsp olive oil
- ½ tsp garlic powder
- Salt and pepper to taste
- 2 pancetta slices, chopped
- 2 celery stalks, chopped
- 1 medium onion, chopped
- 1 tbsp flour
- ¼ cup white wine
- 1 tsp dried rosemary
- 1 bay leaf
- 1 ½ cups heavy cream
- 2 tbsp chopped fresh chervil

Directions:
1. Fry pancetta on Sauté for 5 minutes until crispy. Remove to a paper towel-lined plate and set aside. Sauté the celery and onion in the same fat for 1 minute, stirring until the vegetables soften. Mix in the flour to coat the vegetables. Pour in the wine simmer. Cook for about 1 minute or until reduced by about one-third.
2. Pour in 1 cup water, the reserved mussel liquid, potatoes, salt, rosemary, and bay leaf. Seal the lid and cook on High Pressure for 4 minutes. Do a natural pressure release for 10 minutes. Stir in mussels and heavy cream.
3. Press Sauté and bring the soup to a simmer to heat the mussels through. Discard the bay leaf. Top with pancetta, chervil, cheese, and crackers and serve.

Stuffed Tench With Herbs & Lemon

Servings: 2
Cooking Time: 20 Minutes

Ingredients:
- 1 tench, cleaned, gutted
- 1 lemon, quartered
- 2 tbsp olive oil
- 1 tsp rosemary, chopped
- ¼ tsp dried thyme
- 2 garlic cloves, crushed

Directions:
1. In a bowl, mix olive oil, garlic, rosemary, and thyme. Stir to combine. Brush the fish with the previously prepared mixture and stuff with lemon. Pour 4 cups of water into the Instant Pot, set the steamer tray, and place the fish on top. Seal the lid and cook on Steam for 15 minutes on High Pressure. Do a quick release. Unlock the lid. For a crispier taste, briefly brown the fish in a grill pan.

Dilled Salmon Fillets

Servings: 4
Cooking Time: 25 Minutes

Ingredients:
- 4 salmon fillets
- 1 cup lemon juice
- 2 tbsp butter, softened
- 2 tbsp dill
- Salt and pepper to taste

Directions:
1. Sprinkle the fillets with salt and pepper. Insert the steamer tray and place the salmon on top. Pour in the lemon juice and 2 cups of water. Seal the lid. Cook on Steam for 5 minutes on High.
2. Release the pressure naturally for 10 minutes. Set aside the salmon and discard the liquid. Wipe the pot clean and press Sauté. Add butter and briefly brown the fillets on both sides, about 3-4 minutes. Sprinkle with dill.

Tangy Shrimp Curry

Servings: 4
Cooking Time: 15 Minutes

Ingredients:
- 1 lb shrimp, deveined
- 2 tbsp sesame oil
- 1 onion, chopped
- ½ tsp fresh ginger, grated
- 1 garlic clove, minced
- 1 tsp cayenne pepper
- 1 tbsp lime juice
- 1 cup coconut milk
- 1 tbsp curry powder
- Salt and pepper to taste

Directions:
1. Heat the sesame oil in your Instant Pot on Sauté and cook the onion, garlic, and ginger for 3-4 minutes. Stir in curry powder, cayenne pepper, salt, and pepper and cook for 3 minutes. Pour in coconut milk, shrimp, and 1 cup of water and seal the lid. Select Manual and cook for 4 minutes on Low pressure. Once done, perform a quick pressure release. Drizzle with lime juice and serve.

Lobster Risotto

Servings:4
Cooking Time: 20 Minutes

Ingredients:
- 4 tablespoons butter
- 1 small onion, peeled and finely diced
- 2 cloves garlic, minced
- 1½ cups Arborio rice
- 1 cup chardonnay
- 3 cups vegetable broth
- ½ teaspoon lemon zest
- 3 tablespoons grated Parmesan cheese
- ½ teaspoon salt
- ¼ teaspoon ground black pepper
- Meat from 3 small lobster tails, diced
- ¼ cup chopped fresh parsley

Directions:
1. Press the Sauté button on the Instant Pot and add the butter. Heat until melted. Add onion and stir-fry for 3–5 minutes until translucent. Add garlic and rice and cook for an additional minute. Add white wine and slowly stir unlidded for 5 minutes until liquid is absorbed by the rice.
2. Add broth, lemon zest, Parmesan, salt, and pepper. Lock lid.
3. Press the Rice button. Let pressure release naturally for 10 minutes. Quick-release any additional pressure until float valve drops and then unlock lid.
4. Stir in lobster, garnish with fresh parsley, and serve warm.

Mediterranean Cod With Cherry Tomatoes

Servings: 4
Cooking Time: 20 Minutes

Ingredients:
- 1 lb cherry tomatoes, halved
- 1 bunch fresh thyme sprigs
- 4 fillets cod
- 2 tbsp olive oil
- 1 clove garlic, pressed
- Salt and pepper to taste
- 1 cup white rice
- 1 cup kalamata olives
- 2 tbsp pickled capers

Directions:
1. Line a parchment paper on the basket of the pot. Place about half the tomatoes in a single layer on the paper. Sprinkle with thyme, reserving some for garnish. Arrange cod fillets on top. Sprinkle with some olive oil. Spread the garlic, pepper, salt, and remaining tomatoes over the fish. In the pot, mix rice and 2 cups of water. Lay a trivet over the rice and water.
2. Lower steamer basket onto the trivet. Seal the lid, and cook for 7 minutes on Low Pressure. Release the pressure quickly. Remove the steamer basket and trivet from the pot. Use a fork to fluff the rice. Plate the fish fillets and apply a garnish of olives, reserved thyme, remaining olive oil, and capers. Serve with rice.

Seafood Medley With Rosemary Rice

Servings: 4
Cooking Time: 45 Minutes

Ingredients:
- 1 lb frozen seafood mix
- 1 cup brown rice
- 1 tbsp calamari ink
- 2 tbsp extra virgin olive oil
- 2 garlic cloves, crushed
- 1 tbsp chopped rosemary
- ½ tsp salt
- 3 cups fish stock
- ½ lemon

Directions:
1. Add in seafood mix, rice, calamari ink, olive oil, garlic, rosemary, salt, stock, and lemon, seal the lid and cook on Manual for 25 minutes on High. Release the pressure naturally for 10 minutes. Squeeze lemon juice and serve.

Herby Crab Legs With Lemon

Servings: 4
Cooking Time: 10 Minutes

Ingredients:
- 3 lb king crab legs, broken in half
- 1 tsp rosemary
- 1 tsp thyme
- 1 tsp dill
- ¼ cup butter, melted
- Salt and pepper to taste
- 1 lemon, cut into wedges

Directions:
1. Pour 1 cup of water into your Instant Pot and fit in a trivet. Season the crab legs with rosemary, thyme, dill, salt, and pepper; place on the trivet. Seal the lid, select Manual, and cook for 3 minutes. When ready, perform a quick pressure release. Remove crab legs to a bowl and drizzle with melted butter. Serve with lemon wedges.

Spicy Haddock With Beer & Potatoes

Servings: 4
Cooking Time: 25 Minutes

Ingredients:
- 4 potatoes, cut into matchsticks
- 8 oz beer
- 2 eggs
- 1 cup flour
- ½ tbsp cayenne powder
- 1 tbsp cumin powder
- Salt and pepper to taste
- 4 haddock fillets
- 2 tbsp olive oil

Directions:
1. In a bowl, whisk beer and eggs. In another bowl, combine flour, cayenne, cumin, pepper, and salt. Coat each fish piece in the egg mixture, then dredge in the flour mixture, coating all sides. Grease a baking dish with cooking spray.
2. Place in the fish fillets, pour ¼ cup of water, and grease with cooking spray. Place the potatoes in the pot and cover with water and place a trivet over the potatoes. Lay the baking dish on top and seal the lid. Cook on High Pressure for 15 minutes. Do a quick release. Drain and crush the potatoes with olive oil and serve with the fish.

Octopus & Shrimp With Collard Greens

Servings: 4
Cooking Time: 30 Minutes

Ingredients:
- 6 oz octopus, cut into bite-sized pieces
- 1 lb collard greens, chopped
- 1 lb shrimp, whole
- 1 tomato, chopped
- 3 cups fish stock
- 4 tbsp olive oil
- 3 garlic cloves
- 2 tbsp parsley, chopped
- 1 tsp sea salt

Directions:
1. Place shrimp and octopus in the pot. Add tomato and fish stock. Seal the lid and cook on High Pressure for 15 minutes. Do a quick release. Remove shrimp and octopus. Drain the liquid. Heat olive oil on Sauté and add garlic and parsley and cook for 1 minute. Add in collard greens, season with salt, and simmer for 5 minutes. Serve with shrimp and octopus.

Creamy Wild Salmon

Servings: 4
Cooking Time: 20 Minutes

Ingredients:
- 4 wild sockeye salmon fillets
- 1 tsp dill
- ¼ cup lemon juice
- 4 green onions, sliced
- 1 cup heavy cream
- ¼ cup capers
- 2 tbsp butter
- Salt and pepper to taste

Directions:
1. Sprinkle salmon fillets with dill, salt, pepper, and lemon juice. Pour 1 cup of water into your Instant Pot and fir in a trivet. Place the fillets on the trivet and seal the lid. Select Manual and cook for 5 minutes on High pressure.
2. Once done, perform a quick pressure release and unlock the lid. Remove the salmon and discard the water. Set the pot to Sauté and add in the butter to melt it. Cook the green onions for 3-4 minutes and stir in heavy cream and capers; cook for 2-3 minutes. Taste and adjust the seasoning. Pour the sauce over the salmon and serve.

Paprika Salmon With Dill Sauce

Servings: 2
Cooking Time: 15 Minutes

Ingredients:
- 2 salmon fillets
- ¼ tsp paprika
- Salt and pepper to taste
- ¼ cup fresh dill
- Juice from ½ lemon
- Sea salt to taste
- ¼ cup olive oil

Directions:
1. In a food processor, blend the olive oil, lemon juice, dill, and seas salt until creamy; reserve. To the cooker, add 1 cup water and place a steamer basket. Arrange salmon fillets skin-side down on the steamer basket. Sprinkle the salmon with paprika, salt, and pepper. Seal the lid and cook for 3 minutes on High Pressure. Release the pressure quickly. Top the fillets with dill sauce to serve.

Chili Squid

Servings: 4
Cooking Time: 35 Minutes

Ingredients:
- 1 lb squid, sliced into rings
- 1 tsp onion powder
- 2 tbsp flour
- 1 garlic clove, minced
- 1 tbsp chives
- ¼ tsp chili pepper, chopped
- ¼ tsp smoked paprika
- 1 tbsp lemon juice
- 1 cup vegetable broth
- 2 tbsp butter
- Salt and pepper to taste
- 2 tbsp parsley, chopped

Directions:
1. Mix the onion powder, smoked paprika, flour, garlic, chives, chili pepper, salt, and pepper in a bowl. Add in the squid slices and toss to coat. Let sit for 10 minutes.
2. Melt the butter in your Instant Pot on Sauté. Place in the squid mixture and cook for 3-4 minutes. Pour in the vegetable broth and seal the lid. Cook on Manual for 12 minutes on High. Once done, perform a quick pressure release and unlock the lid. Serve sprinkled with parsley.

Pistachio-crusted Halibut

Servings:2
Cooking Time: 7 Minutes

Ingredients:
- 1 tablespoon Dijon mustard
- 1 teaspoon fresh lemon juice
- 2 tablespoons panko bread crumbs
- ¼ cup chopped unsalted pistachios
- ½ teaspoon salt
- 2 halibut fillets
- 1 cup water

Directions:
1. Preheat the oven to broiler for 500°F.
2. In a small bowl, combine mustard, lemon juice, bread crumbs, pistachios, and salt to form a thick paste.
3. Pat the halibut fillets dry with a paper towel. Rub the paste on the top of each fillet and place in steamer basket.
4. Pour 1 cup water in the Instant Pot. Insert trivet. Place steamer basket on trivet. Lock lid.
5. Press the Manual button and adjust time to 5 minutes. When timer beeps, quick-release the pressure until float valve drops and then unlock lid. Transfer fillets to a parch-

ment-paper-lined baking sheet.

6. Broil for approximately 1–2 minutes until tops are browned. Remove from heat and serve hot.

Shrimp Boil With Chorizo Sausages

Servings: 4
Cooking Time: 15 Minutes

Ingredients:
- 3 red potatoes
- 3 ears corn, cut into rounds
- 1 cup white wine
- 4 chorizo sausages, chopped
- 1 lb shrimp, deveined
- 2 tbsp of seafood seasoning
- Salt to taste
- 1 lemon, cut into wedges
- ¼ cup butter, melted

Directions:
1. Add potatoes, corn, wine, chorizo, shrimp, seafood seasoning, and salt. Do not stir. Add in 2 cups of water. Seal the lid and cook for 2 minutes on High Pressure. Release the pressure quickly. Drain the mixture through a colander. Transfer to a plate. Serve with melted butter and lemon wedges.

Haddock With Edamame Soybeans

Servings: 4
Cooking Time: 25 Minutes

Ingredients:
- 1 pack edamame soybeans
- 1 lb haddock fillets
- 1 clove garlic, minced
- 2 tsp grated ginger
- ¼ red chili, sliced
- 1 tbsp honey
- 2 tbsp soy sauce
- Salt and pepper to taste

Directions:
1. Pour 1 cup of water into your Instant Pot and fit in a trivet. Mix garlic, ginger, red chili, honey, soy sauce, salt, and pepper in a bowl. Add in the haddock fillets and toss to coat. Spread the fillets on a greased baking pan; scatter edamame soybeans around. Place the pan on the trivet.
2. Seal the lid. Cook on Steam for 6 minutes on High pressure. When done, allow a natural release for 10 minutes, then perform a quick pressure release. Serve.

Herby Trout With Farro & Green Beans

Servings: 4
Cooking Time: 20 Minutes

Ingredients:
- 1 cup farro
- 2 cups water
- 4 skinless trout fillets
- 8 oz green beans
- 1 tbsp olive oil
- Salt and pepper to taste
- 4 tbsp melted butter
- ½ tbsp sugar
- ½ tbsp lemon juice
- ½ tsp dried rosemary
- 2 garlic cloves, minced
- ½ tsp dried thyme

Directions:
1. Pour the farro and water into the pot and mix with green beans and olive oil. Season with salt and black pepper. In another bowl, mix the remaining black pepper and salt, butter, sugar, lemon juice, rosemary, garlic, and thyme.
2. Coat the trout with the buttery herb sauce. Insert a trivet in the pot and lay the trout fillets on the trivet. Seal the lid and cook on High Pressure for 12 minutes. Do a quick release and serve immediately.

Beer-steamed Shrimp

Servings:4
Cooking Time: 0 Minutes

Ingredients:
- 1 bottle beer
- 2 pounds jumbo shrimp, peeled and deveined
- 1 medium lemon, quartered
- 2 tablespoons Old Bay Seasoning

Directions:
1. Add beer to the Instant Pot and insert steamer basket. Place shrimp in basket. Squeeze lemons over shrimp and add squeezed wedges for additional aromatics. Lock lid.
2. Press the Steam button and adjust time to 0 minutes. When timer beeps, quick-release pressure until float valve drops. Unlock lid. Discard lemons.
3. Transfer shrimp to a serving dish and toss with Old Bay Seasoning. Serve warm or chilled.

Cheesy Tuna

Servings: 4
Cooking Time: 20 Minutes

Ingredients:
- 1 lb tuna fillets
- 2 tbsp butter
- 1 tbsp flour
- Salt and pepper to taste
- ½ cup milk
- 1 cup mozzarella, grated

Directions:
1. Melt the butter in your Instant Pot on Sauté. Place in flour, salt, and pepper and cook for 1 minute. Pour in milk and cook for 3-5 minutes, stirring often.
2. Stir in mozzarella cheese. Place the tuna fillets in a greased baking pan and pour the cheese sauce over the fish. Cover with aluminium foil.
3. Clean the pot and add 1 cup of water. Fit in a trivet. Place the pan on the trivet and seal the lid. Select Manual and cook for 5 minutes on High pressure. When ready, perform a quick pressure release and unlock the lid.

Mint Salmon On Spinach Bed

Servings: 4
Cooking Time: 15 Minutes

Ingredients:
- 1 lb salmon fillets, boneless
- 1 lb fresh spinach, torn
- 2 tbsp olive oil
- 2 garlic cloves, chopped
- 2 tbsp lemon juice
- 1 tbsp fresh mint, chopped

Directions:
1. Place spinach in the pot, cover with water, and lay the trivet on top. Rub the salmon fillets with half of the olive oil, mint, and garlic. Lay on the trivet. Seal the lid and cook on Steam for 5 minutes on High. Do a quick release. Remove salmon to a serving plate. Drain the spinach. Serve the fish on a bed of spinach. Season with salt and drizzle with lemon juice.

Shrimp Fajitas

Servings:8
Cooking Time: 0 Minutes

Ingredients:
- 2 pounds jumbo shrimp, peeled and deveined
- 2 medium bell peppers (color of choice), seeded and sliced
- 1 medium red onion, peeled and sliced
- 1 packet fajita sauce
- 2 cups water
- 16 flour tortillas, warmed

Directions:
1. In a medium bowl, add shrimp, bell peppers, onion, and fajita sauce. Refrigerate covered 30 minutes.
2. Add water to the Instant Pot and insert steamer basket. Place shrimp and vegetables in basket. Lock lid.
3. Press the Steam button and adjust time to 0 minutes. When timer beeps, quick-release pressure until float valve drops. Unlock lid.
4. Transfer shrimp and vegetables to a serving bowl. Distribute mixture evenly on tortillas. Serve warm.

Basil Clams With Garlic & White Wine

Servings: 4
Cooking Time: 15 Minutes

Ingredients:
- 1 lb clams, scrubbed
- 2 tbsp butter
- 4 green garlic, chopped
- 1 tbsp lemon juice
- ½ cup white wine
- ½ cup chicken stock
- Salt and pepper to taste
- 2 tbsp basil, chopped

Directions:
1. Melt the butter in your Instant Pot on Sauté. Add in the garlic and clams and cook for 3-4 minutes. Stir in lemon juice and chicken stock, white wine, salt, and pepper and seal the lid. Select Manual and cook for 3 minutes on High pressure. Once done, perform a quick pressure release and unlock the lid. Discard unopened clams. Serve topped with basil.

Cheesy Shrimp Scampi

Servings: 4
Cooking Time: 10 Minutes

Ingredients:
- 1 lb shrimp, deveined
- 2 tbsp olive oil
- 1 clove garlic, minced
- 1 tbsp tomato paste
- 10 oz canned tomatoes, diced
- ½ cup dry white wine
- 1 tsp red chili pepper
- 1 tbsp parsley, chopped
- Salt and pepper to taste
- 1 cup Grana Padano, grated

Directions:
1. Warm the olive oil in your Instant Pot on Sauté. Add in garlic and cook for 1 minute. Stir in shrimp, tomato paste, tomatoes, white wine, chili pepper, parsley, salt, pepper, and ¼ cup of water and seal the lid. Select Manual and cook for 3 minutes on High pressure. Once done, perform a quick pressure release and unlock the lid. Serve garnished with Grana Padano cheese.

White Wine Marinated Squid Rings

Servings: 3
Cooking Time: 25 Minutes + Cooling Time

Ingredients:
- 1 lb fresh squid rings
- 1 cup dry white wine
- 1 cup olive oil
- 2 garlic cloves, crushed
- 1 lemon, juiced
- 2 cups fish stock
- ¼ tsp red pepper flakes
- ¼ tsp dried oregano
- 1 tbsp rosemary, chopped
- 1 tsp sea salt

Directions:
1. In a bowl, mix wine, olive oil, lemon juice, garlic, flakes, oregano, rosemary, and salt. Submerge squid rings in this mixture and cover with a lid. Refrigerate for 1 hour. Remove the squid from the fridge and place it in the pot along with stock and half of the marinade. Seal the lid. Cook on High Pressure for 6 minutes. Release the pressure naturally for 10 minutes. Transfer the rings to a plate and drizzle with some marinade to serve.

Louisiana Grouper

Servings:4
Cooking Time: 20 Minutes

Ingredients:
- 2 tablespoons olive oil
- 1 small onion, peeled and diced
- 1 stalk celery, diced
- 1 small green bell pepper, seeded and diced
- 1 can diced tomatoes
- ¼ cup water
- 1 tablespoon tomato paste
- 1 teaspoon honey
- Pinch of dried basil
- 2 teaspoons Creole seasoning
- 4 grouper fillets, rinsed and cut into bite-sized pieces
- ½ teaspoon sea salt
- ¼ teaspoon ground black pepper

Directions:
1. Press Sauté button on Instant Pot. Heat oil and add onion, celery, and bell pepper. Sauté for 3–5 minutes until onions are translucent and peppers are tender.
2. Stir in undrained tomatoes, water, tomato paste, honey, basil, and Creole seasoning.
3. Sprinkle fish with salt and pepper. Gently toss the fish pieces into the sauce in the Instant Pot. Lock lid.
4. Press the Manual button and adjust time to 5 minutes. When timer beeps, quick-release the pressure until float valve drops and then unlock lid.
5. Transfer fish to a serving platter. Press Sauté button on Instant Pot, press Adjust button to change the temperature to Less, and simmer juices unlidded for 10 minutes. Transfer tomatoes and preferred amount of sauce over fish. Serve immediately.

Spicy Salmon With Oregano & Sea Salt

Servings: 4
Cooking Time: 50 Minutes

Ingredients:
- 1 lb fresh salmon fillets, skin on
- ¼ cup olive oil
- ½ cup lemon juice
- 2 garlic cloves, crushed
- 1 tbsp oregano, chopped
- 1 tsp sea salt
- ¼ tsp chili flakes
- 2 cups fish stock

Directions:

1. In a bowl, mix oil, lemon juice, garlic, oregano leaves, salt, and flakes. Brush the fillets with the mixture and refrigerate for 30 minutes. Pour the stock in, and insert the trivet. Pat dry the salmon and place it on the steamer rack. Seal the lid, and cook on Steam for 10 minutes on High. Do a quick release and serve.

Creole Shrimp With Okra

Servings: 2
Cooking Time: 10 Minutes

Ingredients:
- 1 lb shrimp, deveined
- 6 oz okra, trimmed
- 2 tbsp olive oil
- 1 tsp garlic powder
- ½ tsp cayenne pepper
- ½ tbsp Creole seasoning
- Salt and pepper to taste

Directions:

1. Pour 1 cup water into your Instant Pot and fit in a trivet. In a baking dish, combine shrimp, okra, olive oil, garlic powder, cayenne pepper, Creole seasoning, salt, and pepper and mix to combine. Place the dish on the trivet. Seal the lid and cook for 2 minutes on Steam on High. When ready, perform a quick pressure release. Serve.

Mediterranean Cod With Capers

Servings: 4
Cooking Time: 15 Minutes

Ingredients:
- 4 cod fillets, boneless
- ½ cup white wine
- 1 tsp oregano
- Salt and pepper to taste
- ¼ cup capers

Directions:

1. Pour the white wine and ½ cup of water in your Instant Pot and fit in a trivet. Place cod fillets on the trivet.
2. Sprinkle with oregano, salt, and pepper. Seal the lid, select Steam, and cook for 3 minutes on Low. Once ready, perform a quick pressure release. Top the cod with capers and drizzle with the sauce to serve.

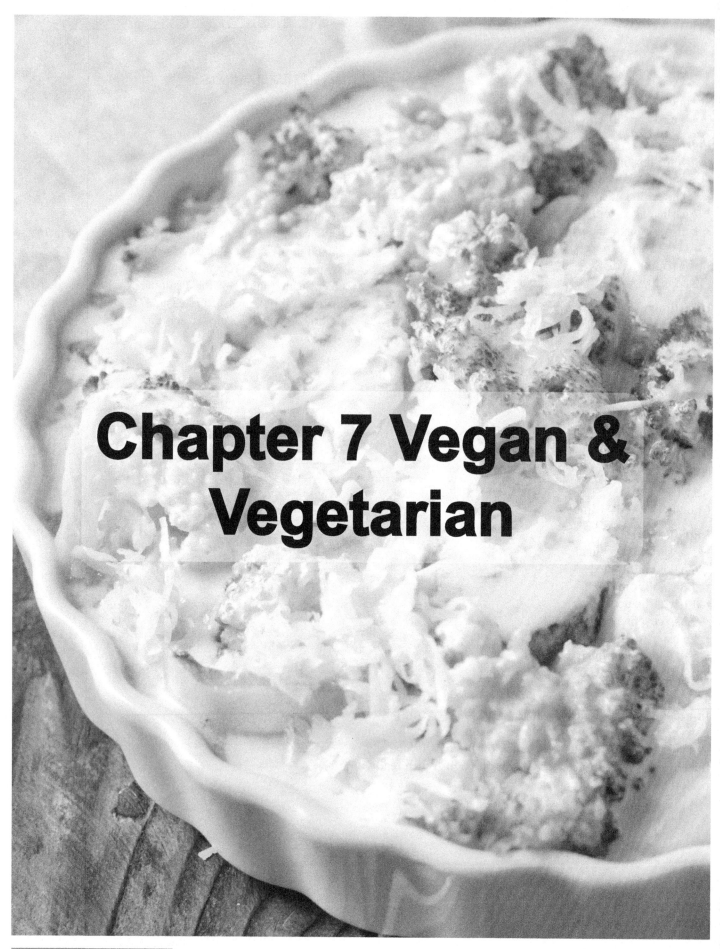

Chapter 7 Vegan & Vegetarian

Sautéed Spinach With Roquefort Cheese

Servings: 2
Cooking Time: 10 Minutes

Ingredients:
- ½ cup Roquefort cheese, crumbled
- 9 oz fresh spinach
- 2 leeks, chopped
- 2 red onions, chopped
- 2 garlic cloves, crushed
- 3 tbsp olive oil

Directions:
1. Grease the inner pot with oil. Stir-fry leeks, garlic, and onions for about 5 minutes on Sauté. Add spinach and give it a good stir. Press Cancel, transfer to a serving dish, and sprinkle with Roquefort cheese. Serve right away.

Quick Cassoulet

Servings:6
Cooking Time: 45 Minutes

Ingredients:
- 1 tablespoon olive oil
- 1 medium yellow onion, peeled and diced
- 2 cups dried cannellini beans, rinsed and drained
- 2 medium carrots, peeled and diced small
- 1 tablespoon Italian seasoning
- 1 teaspoon garlic salt
- ½ teaspoon ground black pepper
- 2 ½ cups vegetable broth
- 1 can diced tomatoes, including juice
- 4 vegan smoked apple sausages, each cut into 4 sections

Directions:
1. Press the Sauté button on the Instant Pot and heat oil. Add onion and stir-fry 3–5 minutes until onions are translucent. Add beans and toss.
2. Add carrots, Italian seasoning, garlic salt, and pepper.
3. Gently pour in broth and diced tomatoes. Press the Cancel button. Lock lid.

4. Press the Bean button and cook for the default time of 30 minutes. When timer beeps, let pressure release naturally for 10 minutes. Quick-release any additional pressure until float valve drops. Press the Cancel button. Unlock lid. Add sausage.
5. Press the Sauté button on the Instant Pot, press the Adjust button to change the temperature to Less, and simmer bean mixture unlidded 10 minutes to thicken. Transfer to a serving bowl and carefully toss. Serve warm.

Millet Eggplant Pilaf

Servings:4
Cooking Time: 17 Minutes

Ingredients:
- 1 tablespoon butter
- ¼ cup peeled and diced onion
- 1 cup peeled and diced eggplant
- 1 small Roma tomato, seeded and diced
- 1 cup millet
- 2 cups vegetable broth
- 1 teaspoon sea salt
- ¼ teaspoon ground black pepper
- ⅛ teaspoon saffron
- ⅛ teaspoon cayenne pepper
- 1 tablespoon chopped fresh chives

Directions:
1. Press Sauté button on Instant Pot. Add butter and melt. Add onion and cook 3–5 minutes until translucent. Toss in eggplant and stir-fry for 2 more minutes. Add diced tomato.
2. Add millet to Instant Pot in an even layer. Gently pour in broth. Lock lid.
3. Press the Rice button. When timer beeps, let pressure release naturally for 5 minutes. Quick-release any additional pressure until float valve drops and then unlock lid.
4. Transfer pot ingredients to a serving bowl. Season with salt, pepper, saffron, and cayenne pepper. Garnish with chives.

Power Green Soup With Lasagna Noodles

Servings: 4
Cooking Time: 25 Minutes

Ingredients:
- 1 tsp olive oil
- 1 cup leeks, chopped
- 2 garlic cloves minced
- 1 cup tomato paste
- 1 cup tomatoes, chopped
- 1 carrot, chopped
- ½ lb broccoli, chopped
- ¼ cup dried green lentils
- 2 tsp Italian seasoning
- Salt to taste
- 2 cups vegetable broth
- 3 lasagna noodles

Directions:
1. Warm olive oil on Sauté. Add garlic and leeks and cook for 2 minutes until soft; add tomato paste, carrot, Italian seasoning, broccoli, tomatoes, lentils, and salt. Stir in vegetable broth and lasagna noodles. Seal the lid and cook on High Pressure for 3 minutes. Release pressure naturally for 10 minutes. Divide into bowls and serve.

Spicy Split Pea Stew

Servings: 4
Cooking Time: 40 Minutes

Ingredients:
- 2 cups split yellow peas
- 1 cup onion, chopped
- 1 carrot, chopped
- 2 potatoes, chopped
- 2 tbsp butter
- 2 garlic cloves, crushed
- 1 tbsp chili pepper
- 4 cups vegetable stock

Directions:
1. Melt butter on Sauté and stir-fry the onion for 3 minutes. Add peas, carrot, potatoes, and garlic and cook for 5-6 minutes until tender. Stir in chili pepper. Pour in the stock and seal the lid. Cook on Meat/Stew for 25 minutes. Do a quick release. Serve.

Curly Kale Soup

Servings: 4
Cooking Time: 20 Minutes

Ingredients:
- 4 cups curly kale
- 2 tbsp Ginger, minced
- 4 Garlic cloves, minced
- 1 tbsp Mustard seeds
- 1 tbsp Olive oil
- 1 cup Heavy cream
- 2 cups vegetable broth
- 1 tbsp Cumin powder

Directions:
1. Warm olive oil in your Instant Pot on Sauté. Place the mustard seeds, garlic, ginger, cumin powder, vegetable broth, curly kale, and heavy cream. Seal the lid, select Manual, and cook for 10 minutes on High pressure. When done, perform a quick pressure release and unlock the lid. Serve warm.

Easy Tahini Sweet Potato Mash

Servings: 4
Cooking Time: 15 Minutes

Ingredients:
- 1 cup water
- 2 lb sweet potatoes, cubed
- 2 tbsp tahini
- ¼ tsp ground nutmeg
- 2 tbsp chopped chives
- Salt and pepper to taste

Directions:
1. Into the cooker, add 1 cup water and insert a steamer basket. Put potato cubes into the steamer basket. Seal the lid and cook for 8 minutes at High Pressure. Release the pressure quickly. In a bowl, add cooked sweet potatoes and slightly mash. Using a hand mixer, whip in nutmeg and tahini until the sweet potatoes attain desired consistency. Add salt and pepper and top with chives.

Parmesan Topped Vegetable Mash

Servings: 6
Cooking Time: 15 Minutes

Ingredients:
- 3 lb Yukon gold potatoes, chopped
- 2 cups cauliflower florets
- 1 carrot, chopped
- 1 cup Parmesan, shredded
- ¼ cup butter, melted
- ¼ cup milk
- 1 tsp salt
- 1 garlic clove, minced
- 2 tbsp parsley, chopped

Directions:
1. Into the pot, add potatoes, cauliflower, carrot and salt; cover with enough water. Seal the lid and cook on High Pressure for 10 minutes. Release the pressure quickly. Drain the vegetables and mash them with a potato masher. Add garlic, butter, and milk. Whisk until well incorporated. Top with Parmesan cheese and parsley.

White Bean Cassoulet

Servings:6
Cooking Time: 45 Minutes

Ingredients:
- 1 tablespoon olive oil
- 1 medium onion, peeled and diced
- 2 cups dried cannellini beans
- 1 medium parsnip, peeled and diced small
- 2 medium carrots, peeled and diced small
- 2 stalks celery, diced
- 1 medium zucchini, diced large
- ½ teaspoon fennel seed
- ¼ teaspoon ground nutmeg
- ½ teaspoon garlic powder
- 1 teaspoon sea salt
- ½ teaspoon ground black pepper
- 2 cups vegetable broth
- 1 can diced tomatoes, including juice
- 2 sprigs rosemary

Directions:
1. Press the Sauté button on Instant Pot. Heat oil Add onion and stir-fry 3–5 minutes until onions are translucent. Add beans and toss.
2. Add a layer of diced parsnips, then a layer of carrots, and next a layer of celery. Finally, add a layer of zucchini. Sprinkle in fennel seed, nutmeg, garlic powder, salt, and pepper.

3. Gently pour in broth and canned tomatoes. Then add rosemary. Lock lid.
4. Press the Bean button and cook for the default time of 30 minutes. When timer beeps, let pressure release naturally for 10 minutes. Quick-release any additional pressure until float valve drops and then unlock lid.
5. Press the Sauté button on the Instant Pot, press the Adjust button to change the temperature to Less, and simmer bean mixture unlidded for 10 minutes to thicken. Transfer to a serving bowl and carefully toss. Discard rosemary and serve.

Zucchini Pomodoro

Servings:4
Cooking Time: 12 Minutes

Ingredients:
- 1 tablespoon avocado oil
- 1 large onion, peeled and diced
- 3 cloves garlic, minced
- 1 can diced tomatoes, including juice
- ½ cup water
- 1 tablespoon Italian seasoning
- 1 teaspoon sea salt
- ½ teaspoon ground black pepper
- 2 medium zucchini, spiraled

Directions:
1. Press Sauté button on the Instant Pot. Heat avocado oil. Add onions and stir-fry for 3–5 minutes until translucent. Add garlic and cook for an additional minute. Add tomatoes, water, Italian seasoning, salt, and pepper. Add zucchini and toss to combine. Lock lid.
2. Press the Manual button and adjust time to 1 minute. When timer beeps, let pressure release naturally for 5 minutes. Quick-release any additional pressure until float valve drops and then unlock lid.
3. Transfer zucchini to four bowls. Press Sauté button, press Adjust button to change the temperature to Less, and simmer sauce in the Instant Pot unlidded for 5 minutes. Ladle over zucchini and serve immediately.

Hot Tofu Meatballs

Servings: 4
Cooking Time: 35 Minutes

Ingredients:
- 1 lb tofu, crumbled
- 2 tbsp butter, melted
- ¼ cup almond meal
- 1 garlic clove, minced
- 2 tbsp olive oil
- 3 tbsp hot sauce
- 2 tbsp chopped scallions
- Salt to taste

Directions:
1. Mix the almond meal, tofu, garlic, salt, and scallions in a bowl. Make meatballs out of the mixture. Warm olive oil in your Instant Pot on Sauté. Place the meatballs and cook for 10 minutes until browned.
2. In the meantime, microwave the butter and hot sauce in a bowl. Combine and set aside. Place the meatballs in the pot and top with hot sauce and 1 cup of water. Seal the lid, select Manual, and cook for 15 minutes on High pressure. When done, perform a quick pressure release and unlock the lid. Serve immediately.

Steamed Artichokes With Lime Aioli

Servings: 4
Cooking Time: 20 Minutes

Ingredients:
- 2 large artichokes
- 2 garlic cloves, smashed
- ½ cup mayonnaise
- Salt and pepper to taste
- Juice of 1 lime

Directions:
1. Using a serrated knife, trim about 1 inch from the top of the artichokes. Into the pot, add 1 cup of water and set trivet over. Lay the artichokes on the trivet. Seal lid and cook for 14 minutes on High Pressure. Release the pressure quickly. Mix the mayonnaise, garlic, and lime juice. Season with salt and pepper. Serve artichokes on a platter with garlic mayo on the side.

Sweet Polenta With Pistachios

Servings: 4
Cooking Time: 20 Minutes

Ingredients:
- ½ cup honey
- 5 cups water
- 1 cup polenta
- ½ cup heavy cream
- ¼ tsp salt
- ¼ cup pistachios, toasted

Directions:
1. Set your Instant Pot to Sauté. Place honey and water and bring to a boil, stirring often. Stir in polenta. Seal the lid, select Manual, and cook for 12 minutes on High.
2. When ready, perform a quick pressure release and unlock the lid. Mix in heavy cream and let sit for 1 minute. Sprinkle with salt to taste. Top with pistachios and serve.

Speedy Mac & Goat Cheese

Servings: 4
Cooking Time: 20 Minutes

Ingredients:
- 1 lb elbow macaroni
- 2 oz goat's cheese, crumbled
- ½ cup skim milk
- 1 tsp Dijon mustard
- 1 tsp dried oregano
- 1 tsp Italian seasoning
- 2 tbsp olive oil
- 5 oz olives, sliced

Directions:
1. Add macaroni in the Instant Pot and cover with water. Seal the lid and cook on High Pressure for 4 minutes. Do a quick release. Drain the macaroni and set aside. Press Sauté on the pot and add the olive oil, mustard, milk, oregano, and Italian seasoning. Cook for 3 minutes. Stir in macaroni and cook for 2 minutes. Top with fresh goat's cheese and olives and serve.

Stuffed Potatoes With Feta & Rosemary

Servings: 4
Cooking Time: 50 Minutes

Ingredients:
- 1 cup button mushrooms, chopped
- 6 whole potatoes
- ¼ cup olive oil
- 3 garlic cloves, minced
- ¼ cup feta cheese
- 1 tsp rosemary, chopped
- ½ tsp dried thyme
- 1 tsp salt

Directions:
1. Rub the potatoes with salt and place them in the Instant Pot. Add enough water to cover and seal the lid. Cook on High Pressure for 30 minutes. Do a quick release and remove the potatoes. Let chill for a while.
2. In the pot, mix oil, garlic, rosemary, thyme, and mushrooms. Sauté until the mushrooms soften, 5 minutes on Sauté. Stir in feta. Cut the top of each potato and spoon out the middle. Fill with cheese mixture and serve.

Homemade Gazpacho Soup

Servings: 4
Cooking Time: 2 Hours 20 Minutes

Ingredients:
- 1 lb trimmed carrots
- 1 lb tomatoes, chopped
- 1 cucumber, peeled, cubed
- ¼ cup olive oil
- 2 tbsp lemon juice
- 1 red onion, chopped
- 2 cloves garlic
- 2 tbsp white wine vinegar
- Salt and pepper to taste

Directions:
1. Add carrots, salt, and enough water to cover the carrots. Seal the lid and cook for 10 minutes on High Pressure. Do a quick release. In a blender, add carrots, cucumber, red onion, pepper, garlic, oil, tomatoes, lemon juice, vinegar, 4 cups of water, and salt. Blend until very smooth. Place gazpacho into a serving bowl, chill while covered for 2 hours. Serve and enjoy!

Celery & Red Bean Stew

Servings: 4
Cooking Time: 25 Minutes

Ingredients:
- 6 oz red beans, cooked
- 2 carrots, chopped
- 2 celery stalks, chopped
- 1 onion, chopped
- 2 tbsp tomato paste
- 1 bay leaf
- 2 cups vegetable broth
- 3 tbsp olive oil
- 1 tbsp salt
- 2 tbsp parsley, chopped
- 1 tbsp flour

Directions:
1. Warm olive oil on Sauté and stir-fry the onion for 3 minutes. Add celery and carrots. Cook for 5 more minutes. Add red beans, bay leaf, salt, and tomato paste. Stir in 1 tbsp of flour and pour in the vegetable broth. Seal the lid and cook on High Pressure for 5 minutes. Do a natural release for about 10 minutes. Sprinkle with some fresh parsley and serve warm.

Coconut Millet Porridge

Servings: 2
Cooking Time: 25 Minutes

Ingredients:
- ½ cup millet
- ½ cup coconut milk
- 2 tbsp coconut flakes
- 1 tbsp honey

Directions:
1. Place millet, milk, and 1/2 cup of water in your Instant Pot. Seal the lid, select Manual, and cook for 10 minutes on High pressure. When over, allow a natural release for 10 minutes and unlock the lid. Drizzle with honey, top with coconut flakes, and serve.

Coconut Milk Millet Pudding

Servings: 4
Cooking Time: 25 Minutes

Ingredients:
- 1 cup millet
- 1 cup coconut milk
- 4 dried prunes, chopped
- Maple syrup for serving

Directions:

1. Place the millet, milk, and prunes in your Instant Pot. Stir in 1 cup water. Seal the lid, select Manual, and cook for 10 minutes on High pressure. When ready, allow a natural release for 10 minutes. Drizzle with maple syrup.

Cali Dogs

Servings:4
Cooking Time: 0 Minutes

Ingredients:
- 2 cups water
- 8 meat-free, plant-based hot dogs
- 8 hot dog buns
- ½ cup alfalfa sprouts
- 1 medium avocado, peeled, pitted, and diced
- ½ cup crumbled goat cheese

Directions:

1. Pour water into the Instant Pot. Add hot dogs. Lock lid.
2. Press the Manual or Pressure Cook button and adjust time to 0 minutes. When timer beeps, quick-release pressure until float valve drops. Unlock lid.
3. Assemble hot dogs by placing them in buns and topping with remaining ingredients. Serve warm.

Easy Cheesy Mac

Servings:4
Cooking Time: 4 Minutes

Ingredients:
- 1 pound elbow macaroni
- ¼ cup unsweetened almond milk
- 1 cup shredded sharp Cheddar cheese
- ½ cup ricotta cheese
- 2 tablespoons unsalted butter
- 1 teaspoon salt
- ½ teaspoon ground black pepper

Directions:

1. Place macaroni in an even layer in the Instant Pot. Pour enough water to come about ¼" over pasta. Lock lid.
2. Press the Manual or Pressure Cook button and adjust time to 4 minutes. When timer beeps, let pressure release naturally for 3 minutes. Quick-release any additional pressure until float valve drops. Unlock lid.
3. Drain any residual water. Add remaining ingredients. Stir in warmed pot until well combined. Serve warm.

Gingery Butternut Squash Soup

Servings: 6
Cooking Time: 25 Minutes

Ingredients:
- 1 lb peeled and diced Butternut Squash
- 2 garlic cloves, minced
- 1 tbsp Ginger powder
- 4 cups Chicken broth
- 1 cup Heavy cream
- 2 tbsp vegetable oil
- Salt and pepper to taste

Directions:

1. Place the vegetable oil and half of the butternut squash cubes and cook for 5 minutes until browns on Sauté. Add in the remaining cubes, garlic, ginger powder, chicken broth, heavy cream, salt, and black pepper. Seal the lid, select Manual, and cook for 10 minutes on High pressure. When done, perform a quick pressure release and unlock the lid. Using an immersion blender, pulse until purée. Serve immediately.

Turmeric Stew With Green Peas

Servings: 4
Cooking Time: 35 Minutes

Ingredients:
- 2 cups green peas
- 1 onion, chopped
- 4 cloves garlic, minced
- 3 oz of olives, pitted
- 1 tbsp ginger, shredded
- 1 tbsp turmeric
- 1 tbsp salt
- 4 cups vegetable stock
- 3 tbsp olive oil

Directions:
1. Heat olive oil on Sauté. Stir-fry the onion and garlic for 2-3 minutes, stirring a few times. Add peas, olives, ginger, turmeric, salt, and stock and press Cancel. Seal the lid, select Manual, and cook on High Pressure for 20 minutes. Once the timer goes off, do a quick release before opening the lid. Serve with a dollop of yogurt.

Savory Spinach With Mashed Potatoes

Servings: 6
Cooking Time: 20 Minutes

Ingredients:
- 3 lb potatoes, peeled
- ½ cup milk
- ⅓ cup butter
- 2 tbsp chopped chives
- Salt and pepper to taste
- 2 cups spinach, chopped

Directions:
1. Cover the potatoes with salted water in your Instant Pot. Seal the lid and cook on High Pressure for 8 minutes. Release the pressure quickly. Drain the potatoes, and reserve the liquid in a bowl. Mash the potatoes. Mix with butter and milk; season with pepper and salt. With reserved cooking liquid, thin the potatoes to attain the desired consistency. Put the spinach in the remaining potato liquid and stir until wilted; Season to taste. Drain and serve with potato mash. Garnish with chives.

Vegetarian Green Dip

Servings: 4
Cooking Time: 15 Minutes

Ingredients:
- 10 oz canned green chiles, drained, liquid reserved
- 2 cups broccoli florets
- 1 green bell pepper, diced
- ¼ cup raw cashews
- ¼ cup soy sauce
- ½ tsp sea salt
- ¼ tsp chili powder
- ¼ tsp garlic powder
- ¼ tsp cumin

Directions:
1. In the pot, add cashews, broccoli, green bell pepper, and 1 cup water. Seal the lid and cook for 5 minutes on High Pressure. Release the pressure quickly. Carefully unlock the lid. Drain water from the pot. Add reserved liquid from canned green chiles, salt, garlic powder, chili powder, soy sauce, and cumin. Use an immersion blender to blitz the mixture until smooth. Stir in chiles and serve.

Bavarian Kale And Potatoes

Servings:4
Cooking Time: 10 Minutes

Ingredients:
- 1 tablespoon olive oil
- 1 small onion, peeled and diced
- 1 stalk celery, diced
- 2 cloves garlic, minced
- 4 medium potatoes, peeled and diced
- 2 bunches kale, washed, deveined, and chopped
- 1½ cups vegetable broth
- 2 teaspoons salt
- ½ teaspoon ground black pepper
- ¼ teaspoon caraway seeds
- 1 tablespoon apple cider vinegar
- 4 tablespoons sour cream

Directions:
1. Press the Sauté button on Instant Pot. Heat oil. Add onion and celery and stir-fry 3–5 minutes until onions are translucent. Add garlic and cook for an additional minute. Add potatoes in an even layer. Add chopped kale in an even layer. Add broth. Lock lid.
2. Press the Manual button and adjust time to 5 minutes. Let the pressure release naturally for 10 minutes. Quick-release any additional pressure until float valve drops and then unlock lid; then drain broth.

3. Stir in salt, pepper, caraway seeds, and vinegar; slightly mash the potatoes in the Instant Pot. Garnish each serving with 1 tablespoon sour cream.

Wheat Berry Salad

Servings:6
Cooking Time: 35 Minutes

Ingredients:
- 3 tablespoons olive oil, divided
- 1 cup wheat berries
- 2¼ cups water, divided
- 2 cups peeled and shredded carrots
- 2 apples, peeled, cored, and diced small
- ½ cup raisins
- 2 tablespoons pure maple syrup
- 2 teaspoons orange zest
- ¼ cup fresh orange juice
- 1 tablespoon balsamic vinegar
- ½ teaspoon salt

Directions:
1. Press Sauté button on Instant Pot. Heat 1 tablespoon oil and add wheat berries. Stir-fry for 4–5 minutes until browned and fragrant. Add 2 cups water. Lock lid.
2. Press the Manual button and adjust time to 30 minutes. When timer beeps, let pressure release naturally for 10 minutes. Quick-release any additional pressure until float valve drops and then unlock lid.
3. Let cool for 10 minutes and drain any additional liquid.
4. Transfer cooled berries to a medium bowl and add remaining ingredients. Refrigerate covered overnight until ready to serve chilled.

Steamed Artichokes & Green Beans

Servings: 4
Cooking Time: 20 Minutes

Ingredients:
- 4 artichokes, trimmed
- ½ lb green beans, trimmed
- 1 lemon, halved
- 1 tbsp lemon zest
- 1 tbsp lemon juice
- 3 cloves garlic, crushed
- ½ cup mayonnaise
- Salt to taste
- 2 tbsp parsley, chopped

Directions:
1. Rub the artichokes and green beans with lemon. Add 1 cup water into the pot. Set steamer rack over water and set steamer basket on top. Add in artichokes and green beans and sprinkle with salt. Seal lid and cook on High Pressure for 10 minutes.
2. Release the pressure quickly. In a mixing bowl, combine mayonnaise, garlic, lemon juice, and lemon zest. Season to taste with salt. Serve with warm steamed artichokes and green beans sprinkled with parsley.

Chapter 8 Beans, Rice, & Grains

Chapter 8 Beans, Rice, & Grains

Boston Baked Beans

Servings:10
Cooking Time: 45 Minutes

Ingredients:
- 1 tablespoon olive oil
- 5 slices bacon, diced
- 1 large sweet onion, peeled and diced
- 4 cloves garlic, minced
- 2 cups dried navy beans
- 4 cups chicken broth
- 2 teaspoons ground mustard
- 1 teaspoon sea salt
- ¼ teaspoon ground black pepper
- ¼ cup molasses
- ½ cup ketchup
- ¼ cup packed dark brown sugar
- 1 teaspoon smoked paprika
- 1 teaspoon Worcestershire sauce
- 1 teaspoon apple cider vinegar

Directions:
1. Press Sauté button on Instant Pot. Heat olive oil. Add bacon and onions. Stir-fry for 3–5 minutes until onions are translucent. Add garlic. Cook for an additional minute. Add beans. Toss to combine.
2. Add broth, mustard, salt, and pepper. Lock lid.
3. Press the Bean button and cook for the default time of 30 minutes. When timer beeps, let pressure release naturally for 10 minutes. Quick-release any additional pressure until float valve drops and then unlock lid.
4. Stir in the molasses, ketchup, brown sugar, smoked paprika, Worcestershire sauce, and vinegar. Press the Sauté button on the Instant Pot, press the Adjust button to change the heat to Less, and simmer uncovered for 10 minutes to thicken the sauce; then transfer to a serving dish and serve warm.

Green Goddess Mac 'n' Cheese

Servings: 4
Cooking Time: 20 Minutes

Ingredients:
- 2 cups kale, chopped
- 2 tbsp cilantro, chopped
- 16 oz elbow macaroni
- 3 tbsp unsalted butter
- 4 cups chicken broth
- 3 cups mozzarella, grated
- ½ cup Parmesan, shredded
- ½ cup sour cream

Directions:
1. Mix the macaroni, butter, and chicken broth in your Instant Pot and seal the lid. Select Manual and cook for 4 minutes on High. When ready, perform a quick pressure release and unlock the lid. Stir in Parmesan and mozzarella cheeses, sour cream, kale, and cilantro. Put the lid and let sit for 5 minutes until the kale wilts. Serve.

Wild Rice Pilaf

Servings: 4
Cooking Time: 20 Minutes

Ingredients:
- 1 cup wild rice
- 2 tbsp butter
- Salt and pepper to taste
- 2 tbsp chives, chopped

Directions:
1. Stir the rice, butter, 2 cups of water, salt, and pepper in your Instant Pot. Seal the lid, select Manual, and cook for 5 minutes on High pressure. When ready, allow a natural release for 10 minutes and unlock the lid. Using a fork, fluff the rice. Top with chives and serve.

Vegetable Paella

Servings: 4
Cooking Time: 37 Minutes

Ingredients:
- 2 tbsp butter
- 1 cup long-grain rice
- 1 ½ cups vegetable stock
- A pinch of saffron
- 1 red bell pepper, chopped
- ½ cup green peas
- 1 cup tomato sauce
- 1 tsp cumin
- 1 tsp chili powder
- ½ tsp garlic powder
- ½ tsp onion powder
- 1 lemon, cut into wedges

Directions:
1. Melt butter in your Instant Pot to Sauté. Add in rice and bell pepper and cook for 2 minutes. Mix in vegetable stock, tomato sauce, cumin, saffron, chili powder, garlic powder, and onion powder. Seal the lid, select Manual, and cook for 10 minutes on High pressure. Once ready, allow a natural release for 10 minutes and unlock the lid. Stir in green peas and cook for 4-5 minutes more on Sauté. Serve with lemon wedges.

Quinoa Bowls With Broccoli & Pesto

Servings: 2
Cooking Time: 15 Minutes

Ingredients:
- 1 bunch baby heirloom carrots, peeled
- 1 cup quinoa
- 2 cups vegetable broth
- Salt and pepper to taste
- 1 potato, peeled, cubed
- 10 oz broccoli florets
- ¼ cabbage, chopped
- 2 eggs
- 1 avocado, sliced
- ¼ cup pesto sauce
- Lemon wedges, for serving

Directions:
1. In your Instant Pot, mix the vegetable broth, pepper, quinoa, and salt. Set a trivet on top of the quinoa and place a steamer basket on the trivet. Mix carrots, potato, eggs, and broccoli in the steamer basket. Seal the lid and cook for 1 minute on High Pressure. Quick-release the pressure. Remove the trivet and basket from the pot.

2. Set the eggs in a bowl of ice water. Then peel and halve them. Fluff the quinoa. In two bowls, equally divide avocado, quinoa, broccoli, eggs, carrots, potato, cabbage, and pesto dollop. Serve with lemon wedges.

Spicy Three-bean Vegetable Chili

Servings: 6
Cooking Time: 40 Minutes

Ingredients:
- 1 tbsp canola oil
- 1 onion, chopped
- 3 stalks of celery, chopped
- 1 cup green peas
- 10 oz broccoli florets
- 2 tbsp minced garlic
- 2 tbsp chili powder
- 2 tsp ground cumin
- 4 cups vegetable broth
- 28-oz can tomatoes, diced
- ½ cup pinto beans, soaked
- ½ cup black beans, soaked
- ½ cup cannellini beans
- Salt to taste
- 2 tbsp parsley, chopped

Directions:
1. Warm oil on Sauté. Add in onion, broccoli, and celery and cook for 5 minutes until softened. Mix in cumin, chili powder, and garlic and cook for another 1 minute. Pour in vegetable broth, tomatoes, green peas, black beans, salt, cannellini beans, and pinto beans and stir. Seal the lid and cook for 25 minutes on High Pressure. Do a quick pressure release. Dispose of the bay leaf. Adjust the seasonings. Sprinkle with parsley and serve.

Ham & Peas With Goat Cheese

Servings: 4
Cooking Time: 40 Minutes

Ingredients:
- 4 goat cheese, crumbled
- 1 cup dried peas, rinsed
- 3 oz ham, diced
- 3 cups vegetable stock
- 1 tsp mustard powder
- Salt and pepper to taste

Directions:
1. Place peas, ham, mustard powder, and vegetable stock in your Instant Pot. Seal the lid, select Manual, and cook for 20 minutes on High. Once done, allow a natural release for

10 minutes and unlock the lid. Sprinkle with salt and pepper to taste. Top with goat cheese slices and serve.

Cheesy Mushrooms With Garganelli

Servings: 4
Cooking Time: 20 Minutes

Ingredients:
- 8 oz garganelli
- 1 tbsp salt
- 1 large egg
- 8 oz Gruyère, shredded
- 2 cups mushrooms, sliced
- 2 tbsp chopped cilantro
- 3 tbsp sour cream
- 2 tbsp butter
- 3 tbsp cheddar, grated

Directions:
1. Put the garganelli, butter, and salt into the pot and cover with water. Seal lid and cook on High Pressure for 4 minutes. Do a quick pressure release. Melt butter on Sauté and cook mushrooms for 5-6 minutes until tender.
2. In a bowl, whisk egg, Gruyère cheese, and sour cream. Add in garganelli and stir in the mushrooms until the cheese melts. Serve sprinkled with cheddar and cilantro.

Lentil-spinach Curry

Servings:4
Cooking Time: 12 Minutes

Ingredients:
- 1 tablespoon olive oil
- ½ cup peeled and diced onion
- 1 clove garlic, minced
- 1 cup yellow lentils
- 4 cups water
- ½ teaspoon ground coriander
- ½ teaspoon ground turmeric
- ½ teaspoon curry powder
- ½ cup diced tomato
- 2 cups fresh spinach

Directions:
1. Press the Sauté button on Instant Pot. Heat olive oil and add onions. Stir-fry 3–5 minutes until onions are translucent. Add garlic and cook for an additional minute. Add lentils and toss to combine. Pour in water. Lock lid.
2. Press the Manual button and adjust time to 6 minutes. When the timer beeps, quick-release the pressure until float valve drops and then unlock lid. Drain any residual liquid. Toss in coriander, turmeric, and curry powder. Stir in toma-

to and fresh spinach.
3. Press Sauté button on the Instant Pot, press Adjust button to change the heat to Less, and simmer unlidded until tomatoes are heated through and spinach has wilted.
4. Transfer to a dish and serve.

Down South Savory Porridge

Servings:4
Cooking Time: 25 Minutes

Ingredients:
- 1 tablespoon bacon grease
- 1 large Vidalia onion, peeled and diced
- 1 cup sliced cooked sausage
- 1 cup jasmine rice
- 1 cup water
- 1 cup vegetable broth
- 1 cup shredded Cheddar cheese

Directions:
1. Press the Sauté button on the Instant Pot and heat bacon grease. Add onion and sausage and cook 3–5 minutes until onions are translucent.
2. Add a level layer of rice. Slowly pour in water and broth. Lock lid.
3. Press the Porridge button and cook for the default time of 20 minutes. When timer beeps, let pressure release naturally for 10 minutes. Quick-release any additional pressure until float valve drops and then unlock lid.

Beef Pasta Alla Parmigiana

Servings: 6
Cooking Time: 20 Minutes

Ingredients:
- 3 tsp olive oil
- 1 ¼ lb ground beef
- 1 cup white wine
- 1 tsp onion powder
- 3 beef bouillon cubes
- 1 lb conchiglie pasta shells
- ½ cup Parmesan, shredded
- Salt and pepper to taste
- 5 basil leaves, torn

Directions:
1. Warm olive oil in your Instant Pot on Sauté. Add in the ground beef and stir-fry until browned, about 5 minutes. Place 3 cups of water, onion powder, and bouillon cubes in a bowl and mix to combine. Pour it into the pot. Add in the white wine, pasta, salt, and pepper and seal the lid. Select Manual and cook for 5 minutes on High. Once ready,

perform a quick pressure release. Sprinkle with Parmesan cheese and basil and serve.

Cajun Red Beans

Servings:4
Cooking Time: 40 Minutes

Ingredients:
- 1 tablespoon olive oil
- ½ small yellow onion, peeled and diced
- 1 small red bell pepper, seeded and diced
- 1 medium stalk celery, diced
- 3 cups vegetable broth
- 1 cup (about ½ pound) dried red kidney beans, rinsed and drained
- 1 teaspoon Cajun seasoning
- ½ teaspoon garlic salt
- 2 teaspoons Italian seasoning

Directions:
1. Press the Sauté button on the Instant Pot and heat oil. Add onion, bell pepper, and celery. Stir-fry 3–5 minutes until onions are translucent. Deglaze pot by adding broth and scraping the bottom and sides of pot.
2. Add beans, Cajun seasoning, garlic salt, and Italian seasoning. Press the Cancel button. Lock lid.
3. Press the Manual or Pressure Cook button and cook for 35 minutes. When timer beeps, let pressure release naturally for 10 minutes. Quick-release any additional pressure until float valve drops. Unlock lid.
4. With a slotted spoon, transfer beans to a serving dish. Serve warm.

Date & Apple Risotto

Servings: 4
Cooking Time: 30 Minutes

Ingredients:
- 1 tbsp butter
- 1 ½ cups Arborio rice
- 1/3 cup brown sugar
- 2 apples, cored and sliced
- 1 cup apple juice
- 2 cups milk
- 1 ½ tsp cinnamon powder
- ½ cup dates, pitted

Directions:
1. Melt butter in your Instant Pot on Sauté and place in rice; cook for 1-2 minutes. Stir in brown sugar, apples, apple juice, milk, and cinnamon. Seal the lid, select Manual, and cook for 6 minutes on High pressure. Once done, allow

a natural release for 6 minutes and unlock the lid. Mix in dates and cover with the lid. Let sit for 5 minutes.

Red Beans And Chorizo

Servings:8
Cooking Time: 35 Minutes

Ingredients:
- 1 cup dried red beans
- 1 tablespoon olive oil
- 1 small onion, peeled and diced
- 1 small green bell pepper, seeded and diced
- 2 stalks celery, diced
- ½ pound chorizo, loose or removed from casing
- 3 cups chicken broth
- 1 can diced tomatoes, including juice
- ½ teaspoon garlic powder
- ½ teaspoon ground cumin
- ½ teaspoon garlic powder
- ½ teaspoon sea salt
- 2 teaspoons Creole seasoning
- 1 cup shredded Cheddar cheese

Directions:
1. Rinse and drain beans.
2. Press the Sauté button on Instant Pot and heat olive oil. Add onion, bell pepper, celery, and chorizo. Stir-fry 3–5 minutes until onions are translucent. Add broth and deglaze the Instant Pot by scraping the sides and bottom of the Instant Pot.
3. Add beans and remaining ingredients. Lock lid.
4. Press the Bean button and cook for the default time of 30 minutes. When timer beeps, let pressure release naturally for 10 minutes. Quick-release any additional pressure until float valve drops and then unlock lid.
5. Using a slotted spoon, transfer beans to a serving bowl. Let cool to thicken and serve.
6. Stir in Cheddar cheese and transfer to four bowls. Serve warm.

Jamaican Cornmeal Porridge

Servings: 4
Cooking Time: 25 Minutes

Ingredients:
- 1 cup cornmeal
- 1 cup coconut milk
- ½ tsp nutmeg, ground
- 1 tsp vanilla extract
- ½ cup condensed milk
- 1 mango, sliced

Directions:
1. Combine 1 cup of water and cornmeal in a bowl and stir. Add 3 cups of water, coconut milk, vanilla, nutmeg, and cornmeal mixture in your Instant Pot. Seal the lid, select Manual, and cook for 6 minutes on High. Once over, allow a natural release for 10 minutes and unlock the lid. Stir in condensed milk. Top with mango and serve.

Easy Red Lentil Dhal With Spinach

Servings: 6
Cooking Time: 35 Minutes

Ingredients:
- 2 tbsp olive oil
- 1 jalapeño pepper, minced
- 1 cup spinach, chopped
- 4 cloves garlic, minced
- 1 tsp fresh ginger, grated
- 1 tbsp cumin seeds
- 1 tbsp coriander seeds
- 1 tsp ground turmeric
- ¼ tsp cayenne pepper
- 1 ½ cups red lentils
- 1 tomato, diced
- ¼ cup lemon juice
- Salt to taste
- 2 tbsp cilantro, chopped
- Natural yogurt for garnish

Directions:
1. Heat oil on Sauté, add cayenne, red jalapeño, ginger, turmeric, cumin, garlic, and coriander, and cook for 3 minutes until seeds become fragrant and begin to pop.
2. Pour in 3 cups water, tomato, and lentils and stir. Seal the lid and cook on High Pressure for 10 minutes. Release pressure naturally for 10 minutes. Stir in spinach.
3. Cook until wilted, 5 minutes. Add lemon juice and season to taste. Garnish with yogurt and cilantro and serve.

Pancetta With Garbanzo Beans

Servings: 6
Cooking Time: 60 Minutes

Ingredients:
- 3 strips pancetta
- 1 onion, diced
- 15 oz can garbanzo beans
- 1 cup apple cider
- 2 garlic cloves, minced
- ½ cup ketchup
- 1 tbsp mustard powder
- Salt and pepper to taste

Directions:
1. Cook pancetta for 5 minutes until crispy on Sauté. Add onion and garlic, and cook for 3 minutes until soft. Mix in garbanzo beans, ketchup, salt, apple cider, mustard powder, 2 cups water, and black pepper. Seal the lid, press Bean/Chili, and cook on High Pressure for 30 minutes. Release pressure naturally for 10 minutes. Serve.

Couscous With Lamb & Vegetables

Servings: 4
Cooking Time: 40 Minutes

Ingredients:
- 2 tbsp olive oil
- 1 large onion, chopped
- 2 garlic cloves, minced
- 1 lb lamb stew meat, cubed
- 3 cups vegetable stock
- 1 carrot, grated
- 1 red bell pepper, chopped
- 1 cup Israeli couscous
- ½ tsp cumin
- Salt and pepper to taste
- 2 tbsp cilantro, chopped
- 4 lemon wedges

Directions:
1. Heat olive oil on Sauté and cook onion, garlic, and lamb for 6-7 minutes. Stir in carrot, bell pepper, and cumin and sauté for another 3 minutes. Pour in vegetable stock and adjust the seasoning with salt and pepper. Close and secure the lid. Select Manual and cook for 10 minutes on High. Once cooking is complete, use a natural release.
2. Add the couscous and select Sauté on Low. Cover with the lid and simmer for 8-10 minutes until the couscous is tender. Select Cancel and let it sit for 2-3 minutes. Fluff and top with cilantro. Serve with lemon wedges.

Coconut Rice Breakfast

Servings: 4
Cooking Time: 25 Minutes

Ingredients:
- 1 cup brown rice
- 1 cup water
- 1 cup coconut milk
- ½ cup coconut chips
- ¼ cup walnuts, chopped
- ¼ cup raisins
- ¼ tsp cinnamon powder
- ½ cup maple syrup

Directions:
1. Place the rice and water in your Instant Pot. Seal the lid, select Manual, and cook for 15 minutes on High. When ready, perform a quick pressure release and unlock the lid. Stir in coconut milk, coconut chips, raisins, cinnamon, and maple syrup. Seal the lid, select Manual, and cook for another 5 minutes on High pressure. When over, perform a quick pressure release. Top with walnuts.

Pomegranate Rice With Vegetables

Servings: 4
Cooking Time: 15 Minutes

Ingredients:
- ¼ cup pomegranate seeds
- 2 tbsp olive oil
- 1 onion, finely chopped
- 2 cloves garlic, minced
- 1 cup basmati rice
- 1 cup sweet corn, frozen
- 1 cup garden peas, frozen
- ¼ tsp salt
- 1 tsp turmeric powder
- 1 ¼ cups vegetable stock

Directions:
1. Warm oil your Instant Pot on Sauté and add onion and garlic; cook for 3 minutes until fragrant. Stir in rice, corn, peas, salt, turmeric, and stock. Seal the lid, select Manual, and cook for 4 minutes on High pressure. When ready, perform a quick pressure release and unlock the lid. With a fork, fluff the rice. Top with pomegranate and serve.

Cheesy Polenta With Sundried Tomatoes

Servings: 4
Cooking Time: 25 Minutes

Ingredients:
- 1 cup sun-dried tomatoes, finely chopped
- 2 tbsp olive oil
- 1 cup onion, diced
- 2 cloves garlic, chopped
- 2 tsp fresh oregano, minced
- 2 tbsp fresh parsley, minced
- 1 tsp kosher salt
- 4 cups vegetable stock
- ¼ cup Parmesan, shredded
- 1 cup polenta

Directions:
1. Warm olive oil in your Instant Pot on Sauté and add in onion and garlic. Cook for 3 minutes until fragrant. Stir in tomatoes, oregano, parsley, salt, and stock. Top with polenta. Seal the lid, select Manual, and cook for 5 minutes on High pressure. When done, allow a natural release for 10 minutes. Top with Parmesan and serve.

Tomato & Mushroom Rotini

Servings: 4
Cooking Time: 35 Minutes

Ingredients:
- 1 lb rotini pasta
- 2 tbsp olive oil
- ½ yellow onion, diced
- 2 garlic cloves, minced
- 16 oz crushed tomatoes
- 1 cup Mushrooms, sliced
- ½ tbsp grated nutmeg
- ¼ cup basil, chopped
- Salt and pepper to taste

Directions:
1. Cover rotini pasta with salted water in your Instant Pot and seal the lid. Select Manual and cook for 4 minutes on High. When done, allow a natural release for 10 minutes, then perform a quick pressure release, and unlock the lid. Drain the pasta and transfer to a bowl.
2. Heat the olive oil on Sauté and cook the onion, mushrooms, and garlic for 3-4 minutes. Stir in tomatoes and nutmeg and simmer for 5-6 minutes. Stir in basil and cooked pasta; adjust the seasoning. Serve.

Spinach-feta Risotto

Servings:4
Cooking Time: 20 Minutes

Ingredients:
- 3 tablespoons olive oil
- 1 small onion, peeled and finely diced
- 2 cloves garlic, minced
- 1½ cups Arborio rice
- 4 cups chicken broth, divided
- 3 tablespoons grated Parmesan cheese
- ½ teaspoon salt
- ¼ teaspoon ground black pepper
- ½ cup julienned spinach
- ¼ cup crumbled feta cheese
- ¼ cup pitted and finely diced kalamata olives

Directions:
1. Press the Sauté button on the Instant Pot and heat the oil. Add the onion and stir-fry for 3–5 minutes until onions are translucent. Add garlic and rice and cook for an additional 1 minute. Add 1 cup broth and stir for 2–3 minutes until it is absorbed by the rice.
2. Add remaining 3 cups broth, Parmesan cheese, salt, and pepper. Lock lid.
3. Press the Manual button and cook for 10 minutes. When timer beeps, let pressure release naturally for 10 minutes. Quick-release any additional pressure until float valve drops and then unlock lid.
4. Stir in spinach and feta cheese. Transfer a to serving dish and garnish with kalamata olives.

Easy Brown Rice With Sunflower Seeds

Servings: 6
Cooking Time: 30 Minutes

Ingredients:
- 1 tbsp toasted sunflower seeds
- 1 ½ cups brown rice
- 3 cups chicken broth
- 2 tsp lemon juice
- 2 tsp olive oil
- Salt and pepper to taste

Directions:
1. Add broth and brown rice. Season with salt and black pepper. Seal the lid, press Manual, and cook on High for 15 minutes. Release the pressure quickly. Do not open the lid for 5 minutes. Use a fork to fluff rice. Add lemon juice, sunflower seeds, and a drizzle of olive oil and serve.

Risotto With Broccoli & Grana Padano

Servings: 6
Cooking Time: 35 Minutes

Ingredients:
- 2 tbsp Grana Padano cheese flakes
- 10 oz broccoli florets
- 1 onion, chopped
- 3 tbsp butter
- 2 cups carnaroli rice, rinsed
- ¼ cup dry white wine
- 4 cups chicken stock
- Salt and pepper to taste
- 2 tbsp Grana Padano, grated

Directions:
1. Warm butter on Sauté. Stir-fry onion for 3 minutes until translucent. Add in broccoli and rice and cook for 5 minutes, stirring occasionally. Pour wine into the pot and scrape away any browned bits of food from the pan.
2. Stir in stock, pepper, and salt. Seal the lid, press Manual and cook on High for 15 minutes. Release the pressure quickly. Sprinkle with grated Grana Padano cheese and stir well. Top with flaked Grana Padano cheese to serve.

Greek-style Navy Beans

Servings: 4
Cooking Time: 45 Minutes

Ingredients:
- 1 cup navy beans, soaked
- 2 spring onions, sliced
- 1 garlic clove, smashed
- 1 tbsp olive oil
- 1 tsp Greek seasoning
- Salt and pepper to taste

Directions:
1. Place beans, 3 cups water, and garlic in your Instant Pot. Seal the lid, select Manual, and cook for 25 minutes on High pressure. Once done, allow a natural release for 10 minutes and unlock the lid. Drain the beans and combine with olive oil, Greek seasoning, salt, and pepper in a bowl. Serve sprinkled with green onions.

Tomato & Feta Pearl Barley

Servings: 4
Cooking Time: 30 Minutes

Ingredients:
- ½ cup sundried tomatoes in oil, chopped
- ½ cup feta, crumbled
- 1 cup pearl barley
- 2 cups chicken broth
- Salt to taste
- 2 tbsp butter, melted

Directions:
1. Place barley, chicken broth, and salt in your Instant Pot. Seal the lid, select Manual, and cook for 25 minutes on High pressure. When done, allow a natural release for 15 minutes and unlock the lid. Mix in tomatoes and top with feta and butter to serve.

Mexican Pinto Beans

Servings: 4
Cooking Time: 45 Minutes

Ingredients:
- 1 chipotle pepper in adobo sauce, minced
- 1 cup dried pinto beans
- 1 tbsp onion powder
- 2 tbsp garlic powder
- 1 tbsp chili powder
- 1 tsp ground cumin
- 1 tsp Mexican oregano
- Salt and pepper to taste
- 2 tbsp cilantro, chopped

Directions:
1. Place pinto beans, onion powder, garlic powder, cumin, chili powder, chipotle pepper, Mexican oregano, salt, and pepper in your Instant Pot. Pour in 3 cups of water. Seal the lid, select Manual, and cook for 25 minutes on High pressure. When ready, allow a natural release for 10 minutes and unlock the lid. Serve topped with cilantro.

Chapter 9 Desserts & Drinks

Carrot Coconut Cake

Servings:4
Cooking Time: 20 Minutes

Ingredients:
- ¼ cup coconut oil, melted
- ½ cup sugar
- 1 large egg
- ½ teaspoon ground cinnamon
- Pinch of ground nutmeg
- ½ teaspoon vanilla extract
- ¼ cup peeled, grated carrot
- ¼ cup unsweetened coconut flakes
- ½ cup all-purpose flour
- ½ teaspoon baking powder
- ¼ cup chopped pecans
- 1 cup water

Directions:
1. In a medium bowl, whisk together oil, sugar, egg, cinnamon, nutmeg, vanilla, carrot, coconut flakes, flour, and baking powder. Do not overmix. Fold in pecans. Pour batter into a greased 6" cake pan.
2. Pour water into the Instant Pot. Set trivet in pot. Place cake pan on top of the trivet. Lock lid.
3. Press the Manual button and adjust time to 20 minutes. When timer beeps, let pressure release naturally for 5 minutes. Quick-release any additional pressure until float valve drops and then unlock lid.
4. Remove cake pan from the pot and transfer to a rack until cool. Flip cake onto a serving platter.

Cinnamon Applesauce

Servings:8
Cooking Time: 8 Minutes

Ingredients:
- 3 pounds apples (any variety), cored and chopped
- 1 teaspoon ground cinnamon
- ½ teaspoon ground allspice
- ½ cup granulated sugar
- ⅛ teaspoon salt
- ½ cup freshly squeezed orange juice
- ⅓ cup water

Directions:
1. Place all ingredients in the Instant Pot.
2. Press the Manual or Pressure Cook button and adjust time to 8 minutes. When timer beeps, quick-release pressure until float valve drops. Unlock lid.
3. Use an immersion blender to blend ingredients in pot until desired consistency is reached. Serve warm or cold.

Stuffed Apples

Servings:4
Cooking Time: 10 Minutes

Ingredients:
- 4 Granny Smith apples
- 5 tablespoons unsalted butter, softened
- 2 teaspoons ground cinnamon
- ¼ cup packed light brown sugar
- ¼ teaspoon vanilla extract
- ¼ cup chopped walnuts
- ⅛ teaspoon salt
- 2 cups water

Directions:
1. Core apples, leaving some skin on bottom of hole to hold filling in place. Using a paring knife, remove just a little more of the apple center for a bigger area to fill.
2. In a medium bowl, combine butter, cinnamon, brown sugar, vanilla, walnuts, and salt. Stuff apples with this mixture. Place apples in a 7-cup baking dish.
3. Add water to the Instant Pot and insert steam rack. Place

baking dish on steam rack.

4. Press the Manual or Pressure Cook button and adjust time to 10 minutes. When timer beeps, quick-release pressure until float valve drops. Unlock lid.

5. Allow apples to cool in pot 20 minutes. Serve warm.

Amazing Fruity Cheesecake

Servings: 6
Cooking Time: 35 Minutes

Ingredients:
- 1 ½ cups graham cracker crust
- 1 cup raspberries
- 3 cups cream cheese
- 1 tbsp fresh orange juice
- 3 eggs
- ½ stick butter, melted
- ¾ cup sugar
- 1 tsp vanilla paste
- 1 tsp orange zest

Directions:
1. Insert the tray into the pressure cooker, and add 1 cup of water. Grease a springform. Mix in graham cracker crust with sugar and butter in a bowl. Press the mixture to form a crust at the bottom. Blend the raspberries and cream cheese with an electric mixer. Crack in the eggs and keep mixing until well combined. Mix in orange juice, vanilla paste, and orange zest. Pour this mixture into the pan, and cover the pan with aluminum foil. Lay the springform on the tray. Select Pressure Cook and cook for 20 minutes on High. Once the cooking is complete, do a quick pressure release. Refrigerate the cheesecake.

Hot Cocoa Brownies

Servings:6
Cooking Time: 25 Minutes

Ingredients:
- 2 large eggs, beaten
- ¼ cup all-purpose flour
- 2 packets instant hot cocoa mix
- ⅓ cup granulated sugar
- 2 teaspoons baking powder
- 1 teaspoon baking soda
- ⅛ teaspoon salt
- 4 tablespoons unsalted butter, melted
- ⅓ cup mini marshmallows
- 1 cup water

Directions:
1. Grease a 6" cake pan.

2. In a large bowl, combine eggs, flour, hot cocoa mix, sugar, baking powder, baking soda, and salt. Stir in butter and then fold in mini marshmallows. Do not overmix. Pour batter into prepared cake pan.

3. Add water to the Instant Pot and insert steam rack. Place cake pan on top of steam rack. Lock lid.

4. Press the Manual or Pressure Cook button and adjust time to 25 minutes. When timer beeps, let pressure release naturally for 10 minutes. Quick-release any additional pressure until float valve drops. Unlock lid.

5. Remove cake pan from pot and transfer to a cooling rack to cool 10 minutes.

6. Flip brownies onto a serving platter. Let cool completely 30 minutes. Slice and serve.

Cottage Cheesecake With Strawberries

Servings: 6
Cooking Time: 35 Minutes +cooling Time

Ingredients:
- 10 oz cream cheese
- ¼ cup sugar
- ½ cup cottage cheese
- 1 lemon, zested and juiced
- 2 eggs, cracked into a bowl
- 1 tsp lemon extract
- 3 tbsp sour cream
- 1 cup water
- 10 strawberries, halved to decorate

Directions:
1. Blend with an electric mixer, the cream cheese, quarter cup of sugar, cottage cheese, lemon zest, lemon juice, and lemon extract until a smooth consistency is formed. Adjust the sweet taste to liking with more sugar. Add the eggs. Fold in at low speed until incorporated. Spoon the mixture into a greased baking pan. Level the top with a spatula and cover with foil. Fit a trivet in the pot and pour in water. Place the cake pan on the trivet.

2. Seal the lid. Select Manual and cook for 15 minutes. Mix the sour cream and 1 tbsp of sugar. Set aside. Once the timer has gone off, do a natural pressure release for 10 minutes. Use a spatula to spread the sour cream mixture on the warm cake. Let cool. Top with strawberries.

Chocolate Glazed Cake

Servings: 6
Cooking Time: 40 Minutes + Chilling Time

Ingredients:
- 3 cups yogurt
- 3 cups flour
- 2 cups granulated sugar
- 1 cup oil
- 2 tsp baking soda
- 3 tbsp cocoa
- For the glaze:
- 7 oz dark chocolate
- 10 tbsp sugar
- 10 tbsp milk
- 5 oz butter, unsalted

Directions:

1. In a bowl, combine yogurt, flour, sugar, oil, baking soda, and cocoa. Beat well with an electric mixer. Transfer a mixture to a large springform pan. Wrap the pan in foil. Insert a trivet in the Instant Pot. Pour in 1 cup water and place the pan on top. Seal the lid and cook for 30 minutes on High Pressure. Do a quick release, remove the pan, and unwrap. Chill well. Microwave the chocolate and whisk in butter, milk, and sugar. Beat well with a mixer and pour the mixture over the cake. Refrigerate for at least two hours before serving.

Banana Bread Pudding

Servings:4
Cooking Time: 20 Minutes

Ingredients:
- 4 cups cubed French bread, dried out overnight
- 2 small bananas, peeled and sliced
- ¼ cup granulated sugar
- 2 cups whole milk
- 3 large eggs
- ⅛ teaspoon salt
- 3 tablespoons unsalted butter, cut into 4 pats
- 1 ½ cups water

Directions:

1. Grease a 7-cup glass baking dish. Add bread, then banana slices. Sprinkle sugar evenly over bananas. Set aside.
2. In a small bowl, whisk together milk, eggs, and salt. Pour over ingredients in glass baking dish and place butter pats on top.
3. Add water to the Instant Pot and insert steam rack. Place glass baking dish on top of steam rack. Lock lid.
4. Press the Manual or Pressure Cook button and adjust

time to 20 minutes. When timer beeps, quick-release pressure until float valve drops. Unlock lid.
5. Remove glass bowl from pot. Transfer to a cooling rack for 30 minutes until set. Serve.

Banana & Walnut Oatmeal

Servings: 2
Cooking Time: 20 Minutes

Ingredients:
- 1 banana, chopped
- 1 cup rolled oats
- 1 cup milk
- ¼ teaspoon cinnamon
- 1 tbsp chopped walnuts
- ½ tsp white sugar

Directions:

1. Pour 1 cup of water into your Instant Pot and fit in a steam rack. Place oats, sugar, milk, cinnamon, and ½ of water in a bowl. Divide between small-sized cups. Place on the steam rack. Seal the lid, select Manual, and cook for 5 minutes on High pressure. When done, allow a natural release for 10 minutes and unlock the lid. Top with banana and walnuts and serve.

Pie Cups With Fruit Filling

Servings: 6
Cooking Time: 40 Minutes + Chilling Time

Ingredients:
- For the crust:
- 2 cups flour
- ¾ tsp salt
- ¾ cup butter, softened
- 1 tbsp sugar
- ½ cup ice water
- For the filling:
- ½ fresh peach
- ½ cup apples, chopped
- ¼ cup cranberries
- 2 tbsp flour
- 1 tbsp sugar
- ½ tsp cinnamon
- 1 egg yolk, for brushing

Directions:

1. Place flour, salt, butter, sugar, and water in a food processor and pulse until dough becomes crumbly. Remove to a lightly floured work surface. Divide among 4 equal pieces and wrap in plastic foil. Refrigerate for an hour. Place apples, peach, cranberries, flour, sugar, and cinnamon in a

bowl. Toss to combine and set aside. Roll each piece into 6-inch round discs. Add 2 tablespoons of the apple mixture at the center of each disc and wrap to form small bowls. Brush each bowl with egg yolk and gently Transfer to an oiled baking dish. Pour 1 cup of water into the pot and insert the trivet. Place the pan on top. Seal the lid, and cook for 25 minutes on High Pressure. Release the pressure naturally. Serve cool.

Simple Apple Cinnamon Dessert

Servings: 6
Cooking Time: 30 Minutes

Ingredients:
- Topping:
- ½ cup rolled oats
- ½ cup oat flour
- ½ cup granulated sugar
- ¼ cup olive oil
- Filling:
- 5 apples, cored, and halved
- 2 tbsp arrowroot powder
- ½ cup water
- 1 tsp ground cinnamon
- ¼ tsp ground nutmeg
- ½ tsp vanilla paste

Directions:
1. In a bowl, combine sugar, oat flour, rolled oats, and olive oil to form coarse crumbs. Spoon the apples into the Instant Pot. Mix water with arrowroot powder in a bowl. Stir in nutmeg, cinnamon, and vanilla. Toss in the apples to coat. Apply oat topping to the apples. Seal the lid and cook on High Pressure for 10 minutes. Release the pressure naturally for 10 minutes.

Root Beer Float Cupcakes

Servings:12
Cooking Time: 18 Minutes

Ingredients:
- Cupcakes
- ½ box moist vanilla cake mix
- 6 ounces (½ can) root beer
- 2 cups water
- Vanilla Buttercream
- 1 cup confectioners' sugar
- ⅓ cup unsalted butter, softened
- ½ teaspoon vanilla extract
- 1 tablespoon whole milk

Directions:

1. Grease twelve silicone cupcake liners.
2. In a medium bowl, combine cake mix and root beer. Spoon mixture into cupcake liners.
3. Add water to the Instant Pot and insert steam rack. Place six cupcake liners on steam rack. Lock lid.
4. Press the Manual or Pressure Cook button and adjust time to 9 minutes. When timer beeps, quick-release pressure until float valve drops. Unlock lid. Transfer cupcakes to a cooling rack. Repeat cooking process with remaining six cupcake liners.
5. To make buttercream, cream together vanilla buttercream ingredients in a medium mixing bowl. If buttercream is too loose, add a little more confectioners' sugar. If buttercream is too thick, add a little more milk.
6. Let cupcakes cool for at least 30 minutes until they reach room temperature, then spread buttercream on cooled cupcakes. Serve.

Easy Lemon Cake

Servings: 6
Cooking Time: 30 Minutes

Ingredients:
- 2 eggs
- 2 cups sugar
- 1 cup vegetable oil
- ½ cup flour
- 1 tsp baking powder
- Lemon topping:
- 1 cup sugar
- 1 cup lemon juice
- 1 tbsp lemon zest
- 1 lemon, sliced

Directions:
1. In a bowl, combine eggs, sugar, oil, and baking powder. Gradually add flour until the mixture is thick and slightly sticky. Shape balls with hands and flatten them to half-inch thick. Place in a baking pan. Pour 1 cup of water, insert a trivet, and lower the pan onto the trivet. Cover the pan with foil and seal the lid. Cook on High Pressure for 20 minutes. Do a quick release. Let cool at room temperature. Add sugar, lemon juice, lemon zest, and lemon slices to the Instant Pot. Press Sauté and stir until the sugar dissolves. Pour the hot topping over the cake.

Spiced Peaches With Cinnamon Whipped Cream

Servings:6
Cooking Time: 8 Minutes

Ingredients:
- 1½ cups heavy whipping cream
- 2 tablespoons powdered sugar
- 1 teaspoon ground cinnamon
- ½ teaspoon vanilla extract
- 2 cans sliced peaches in syrup
- ¼ cup water
- 2 tablespoons packed light brown sugar
- 1 tablespoon white wine vinegar
- ⅛ teaspoon ground allspice
- 1 teaspoon ground ginger
- 1 cinnamon stick
- 4 whole cloves
- Pinch of cayenne pepper
- 3 whole black peppercorns

Directions:
1. Pour whipping cream into a metal bowl. Whisk until soft peaks form. Slowly add powdered sugar, cinnamon, and vanilla and continue whipping until firm. Set aside and refrigerate.
2. Add remaining ingredients to Instant Pot. Stir to mix. Lock lid.
3. Press the Manual button and adjust time to 3 minutes. When timer beeps, quick-release pressure until float valve drops and then unlock lid. Remove and discard the cinnamon stick, cloves, and peppercorns. Press Sauté button on Instant Pot, press Adjust button to change the temperature to Less, and simmer for 5 minutes to thicken the syrup. Serve warm or chilled, topped with cinnamon whipped cream.

Lemon-apricot Compote

Servings: 6
Cooking Time: 20 Minutes

Ingredients:
- 2 lb fresh apricots, sliced
- 1 lb sugar
- 2 tbsp lemon zest
- 1 tsp ground nutmeg
- 10 cups water

Directions:
1. Add apricots, sugar, water, nutmeg, and lemon zest. Cook, stirring occasionally until half of the water evaporates, on Sauté. Press Cancel and transfer the apricots and

the remaining liquid into glass jars. Let cool. Refrigerate.

Grandma's Fruit Compote

Servings: 6
Cooking Time: 45 Minutes

Ingredients:
- 7 oz Turkish figs
- 7 oz fresh cherries
- 7 oz plums
- 3 ½ oz raisins
- 3 large apples, chopped
- 3 tbsp cornstarch
- 1 tsp cinnamon, ground
- 1 cup sugar
- 1 lemon, juiced

Directions:
1. Combine figs, cherries, plums, raisins, apples, cornstarch, cinnamon, sugar, and lemon juice in the Instant Pot. Pour in 3 cups water. Seal the lid and cook for 30 minutes on High pressure. Release the pressure naturally for 10 minutes. Store in big jars.

Vanilla Cheesecake With Cranberry Filling

Servings: 8
Cooking Time: 1 Hour + Chilling Time

Ingredients:
- 1 cup coarsely crumbled cookies
- 2 tbsp butter, melted
- 1 cup mascarpone cheese
- ½ cup sugar
- 2 tbsp sour cream
- ½ tsp vanilla extract
- 2 eggs
- 1/3 cup dried cranberries

Directions:
1. Fold a 20-inch piece of aluminum foil in half lengthwise twice and set on the Instant Pot. In a bowl, combine butter and crumbled cookies. Press firmly to the bottom and about 1/3 of the way up the sides of a cake pan. Freeze the crust. In a separate bowl, beat mascarpone cheese and sugar to obtain a smooth consistency. Stir in vanilla and sour cream. Beat one egg and add into the cheese mixture to combine well. Do the same with the second egg.
2. Stir cranberries into the filling. Transfer the filling into the crust. Into the pot, add 1 cup water and set the steam rack. Center the springform pan onto the prepared foil sling.

Use the sling to lower the pan onto the rack.

3. Fold foil strips out of the way of the lid. Seal the lid, press Manual, and cook on High Pressure for 40 minutes. Release the pressure quickly. Transfer the cheesecake to a refrigerator for 3 hours. Use a paring knife to run along the edges between the pan and cheesecake to remove the cheesecake and set to the plate.

Spiced & Warming Mulled Wine

Servings: 6
Cooking Time: 20 Minutes

Ingredients:
- 3 cups red wine
- 2 tangerines, sliced
- ¼ cup honey
- 6 whole cloves
- 6 whole black peppercorns
- 2 cardamom pods
- 8 cinnamon sticks
- 1 tsp fresh ginger, grated
- 1 tsp ground cinnamon

Directions:
1. Add red wine, honey, cardamom, 2 cinnamon sticks, cloves, tangerine slices, ginger, and peppercorns. Seal the lid and cook for 5 minutes on High Pressure. Release pressure naturally for 10 minutes. Using a fine mesh strainer, strain the wine. Discard spices. Divide the warm wine into glasses. Garnish with cinnamon sticks to serve.

Chocolate Custard

Servings:4
Cooking Time: 20 Minutes

Ingredients:
- 4 large egg yolks
- 2 tablespoons sugar
- Pinch of salt
- ¼ teaspoon vanilla extract
- 1½ cups half-and-half
- ¾ cup semisweet chocolate chips
- 2 cups water

Directions:
1. In a small bowl, whisk together egg yolks, sugar, salt, and vanilla. Set aside.
2. In saucepan over medium-low heat, heat half-and-half to a low simmer. Whisk a spoonful into the egg mixture to temper the eggs, then slowly add the egg mixture back into the saucepan with remaining half-and-half. Add chocolate chips and continually stir on simmer until chocolate is melt-

ed, about 10 minutes. Remove from heat and evenly distribute chocolate mixture among four custard ramekins.
3. Pour water into Instant Pot. Insert trivet. Place silicone steamer basket onto trivet. Place ramekins onto steamer basket. Lock lid.
4. Press the Manual button and adjust time to 6 minutes. When timer beeps, let pressure release naturally for 10 minutes. Quick-release any additional pressure until float valve drops and then unlock lid.
5. Transfer custards to a plate and refrigerate covered for 2 hours. Serve.

Rice Pudding

Servings:4
Cooking Time: 25 Minutes

Ingredients:
- 1 cup Arborio rice
- 1 ½ cups water
- 1 tablespoon vanilla extract
- 1 cinnamon stick
- 1 tablespoon unsalted butter
- 1 cup golden raisins
- ¼ cup granulated sugar
- ½ cup heavy cream

Directions:
1. Add rice, water, vanilla, cinnamon stick, and butter to the Instant Pot. Lock lid.
2. Press the Manual or Pressure Cook button and adjust time to 20 minutes. When timer beeps, let pressure release naturally for 10 minutes. Quick-release any additional pressure until float valve drops. Press the Cancel button. Unlock lid.
3. Remove cinnamon stick and discard. Stir in raisins, sugar, and heavy cream.
4. Press the Sauté button on the Instant Pot, press Adjust button to change temperature to Less, and simmer unlidded 5 minutes. Serve warm.

Orange New York Cheesecake

Servings: 6
Cooking Time: 1 Hour + Freezing Time

Ingredients:
- For the crust
- 1 cup graham crackers crumbs
- 2 tbsp butter, melted
- 1 tsp sugar
- For the filling
- 2 cups cream cheese
- ½ cup sugar
- 1 tsp vanilla extract
- Zest from 1 orange
- A pinch of salt
- 2 eggs

Directions:
1. Fold a 20-inch piece of aluminum foil in half lengthwise twice and set on the Instant Pot. Grease a parchment paper and line it to a cake pan. In a bowl, combine melted butter, sugar, and graham crackers. Press into the bottom and about ⅓ up the sides of the pan. Transfer the pan to the freezer as you prepare the filling.
2. In a separate bowl, beat sugar, cream cheese, salt, orange zest, and vanilla until smooth. Beat eggs into the filling, one at a time. Stir until combined. Add the filling over the chilled crust in the pan. Add 1 cup water and set a trivet into the pot. Put the pan on the trivet.
3. Seal the lid, press Cake, and cook for 40 minutes on High. Release the pressure quickly. Cool the cheesecake and then transfer it to the refrigerator for 3 hours. Use a paring knife to run along the edges between the pan and cheesecake to remove the cheesecake and set to the plate.

Steamed Bread Pudding

Servings:6
Cooking Time: 20 Minutes

Ingredients:
- 4 cups cubed cinnamon-raisin bread, dried out overnight
- 1 apple, peeled, cored, and diced small
- ¼ cup raisins
- 2 cups whole milk
- 3 large eggs
- ½ teaspoon vanilla extract
- 2 tablespoons pure maple syrup
- ¼ teaspoon ground cinnamon
- Pinch of ground nutmeg
- Pinch of sea salt
- 3 tablespoons butter, cut into 3 pats
- 1½ cups water

Directions:
1. Grease a 7-cup glass dish. Add bread, apple, and raisins. Set aside.
2. In a small bowl, whisk together milk, eggs, vanilla, maple syrup, cinnamon, nutmeg, and salt. Pour over bread in glass dish and place pats of butter on top.
3. Pour water into Instant Pot. Set trivet in pot. Place glass dish on top of trivet. Lock lid.
4. Press the Manual button and adjust time to 20 minutes. When timer beeps, quick-release pressure until float valve drops and then unlock lid.
5. Remove glass bowl from the Instant Pot. Transfer to a rack until cooled. Serve.

Cinnamon Brown Rice Pudding

Servings:4
Cooking Time: 25 Minutes

Ingredients:
- 1 cup short-grain brown rice
- 1⅓ cups water
- 1 tablespoon vanilla extract
- 1 cinnamon stick
- 1 tablespoon butter
- 1 cup raisins
- 3 tablespoons honey
- ½ cup heavy cream

Directions:
1. Add rice, water, vanilla, cinnamon stick, and butter to Instant Pot. Lock lid.
2. Press the Manual button and adjust time to 20 minutes. When timer beeps, let pressure release naturally for 10 minutes. Quick-release any additional pressure until float valve drops and then unlock lid.
3. Remove the cinnamon stick and discard. Stir in the raisins, honey, and cream.
4. Press Sauté button on Instant Pot, press Adjust button to change the temperature to Less, and simmer unlidded for 5 minutes. Serve warm.

Homemade Spanish-style Horchata

Servings: 4
Cooking Time: 20 Minutes

Ingredients:
- 4 cups cold water
- ½ cup short-grain rice
- ¼ stick cinnamon
- Zest from 1 lemon
- 2 tbsp sugar
- 1 tbsp cinnamon powder

Directions:
1. In the pot, combine cinnamon stick, rice and 2 cups of water. Seal the lid cook on High Pressure for 5 minutes. Release pressure naturally for 10 minutes. In a blender, puree the rice mixture with the lemon zest and sugar. Strain the blended mixture into the remaining water. Mix well and place in the refrigerator until ready for serving. Serve sprinkled with cinnamon.

Plum & Almond Dessert

Servings: 6
Cooking Time: 1 Hour 50 Minutes

Ingredients:
- 6 lb sweet ripe plums, pits removed and halved
- 2 cups white sugar
- 1 cup almond flakes

Directions:
1. Drizzle the plums with sugar. Toss to coat. Let it stand for about 1 hour to allow plums to soak up the sugar. Transfer the plum mixture to the Instant Pot and pour 1 cup of water. Seal the lid and cook on High Pressure for 30 minutes. Allow the Pressure to release naturally for 10 minutes. Serve topped with almond flakes.

Walnut & Pumpkin Tart

Servings: 6
Cooking Time: 70 Minutes

Ingredients:
- 1 cup packed shredded pumpkin
- 3 eggs
- ½ cup sugar
- 1 cup flour
- ½ cup half-and-half
- ¼ cup olive oil
- 1 tsp baking powder
- 1 tsp vanilla extract
- 1 tsp ground cinnamon
- ½ tsp ground nutmeg
- ½ cup chopped walnuts
- 2 cups water
- Frosting:
- 4 oz cream cheese, room temperature
- 8 tbsp butter
- ½ cup confectioners sugar
- ½ tsp vanilla extract
- ½ tsp salt

Directions:
1. In a bowl, beat eggs and sugar to get a smooth mixture. Mix in oil, flour, vanilla extract, cinnamon, half-and-half, baking powder, and nutmeg. Stir well to obtain a fluffy batter. Fold walnuts and pumpkin through the batter. Add batter into a cake pan and cover with aluminum foil. Into the pot, add 1 cup water and set a trivet. Lay cake pan onto the trivet.
2. Seal the lid, select Manual, and cook on High Pressure for 40 minutes. Release pressure naturally for 10 minutes. Beat cream cheese, confectioners' sugar, salt, vanilla, and butter in a bowl until smooth. Place in the refrigerator until needed. Remove cake from the pan and transfer to a wire rack to cool. Over the cake, spread frosting and apply a topping of shredded carrots.

Molten Chocolate Cake

Servings: 6
Cooking Time: 40 Minutes

Ingredients:
- 1 cup butter
- 4 tbsp milk
- 2 tsp vanilla extract
- 1 ½ cups chocolate chips
- 1 ½ cups sugar
- Powdered sugar to garnish
- 7 tbsp flour
- 5 eggs
- 1 cup water

Directions:

1. Grease the cake pan with cooking spray and set aside. Fit the trivet at the pot, and pour in water. In a heatproof bowl, add the butter and chocolate and melt them in the microwave for about 2 minutes. Stir in sugar. Add eggs, milk, and vanilla extract and stir again. Finally, add the flour and stir it until smooth. Pour the batter into the greased cake pan and use a spatula to level it. Place the pan on the trivet, inside the pot, seal the lid, and select Manual at High for 15 minutes.

2. Do a natural pressure release for 10 minutes. Remove the trivet with the pan on it and place the pan on a flat surface. Put a plate over the pan and flip the cake over onto the plate. Pour the powdered sugar in a fine sieve and sift over the cake. Cut the cake into slices and serve.

Yogurt Cheesecake With Cranberries

Servings: 6
Cooking Time: 45 Minutes + Chilling Time

Ingredients:
- 2 lb Greek yogurt
- 2 cups sugar
- 4 eggs
- 2 tsp lemon zest
- 1 tsp lemon extract
- 1 cheesecake crust
- For topping:
- 7 oz dried cranberries
- 2 tbsp cranberry jam
- 2 tsp lemon zest
- 1 tsp vanilla sugar
- 1 tsp cranberry extract
- ¾ cup lukewarm water

Directions:

1. In a bowl, combine yogurt, sugar, eggs, lemon zest, and lemon extract. With a mixer, beat well until well-combined. Place the crust in a greased cake pan and pour in the filling. Flatten the surface with a spatula. Leave in the fridge for 30 minutes. Combine cranberries, jam, lemon zest, vanilla sugar, cranberry extract, and water in the pot. Simmer for 15 minutes on Sauté. Remove and wipe the pot clean. Fill in 1 cup water and insert a trivet. Set the pan on top of the trivet and pour cranberry topping. Seal the lid and cook for 20 minutes on High Pressure. Do a quick release. Run a sharp knife around the edge of the cheesecake. Refrigerate. Serve and enjoy!

A

Amazing Fruity Cheesecake   76
Aromatic Lamb Stew   24
Awesome Chicken In Tikka Masala Sauce   37

B

Bacon Cheddar Scrambled Egg Muffins   12
Bacon-poblano Morning Taters   13
Banana & Vanilla Pancakes   16
Banana & Walnut Oatmeal   77
Banana Bread Pudding   77
Basil Clams With Garlic & White Wine   53
Bavarian Kale And Potatoes   63
Bbq Pork Lettuce Cups   45
Beef Meatballs With Tomato-basil Sauce   46
Beef Neapolitan Ragù   46
Beef Pasta Alla Parmigiana   68
Beef Tikka Masala   41
Beer-steamed Shrimp   52
Bell Pepper & Chicken Stew   33
Best Italian Chicken Balls   36
Best Pork Chops With Bbq Sauce & Veggies   41
Boston Baked Beans   66
Breakfast Frittata   15
Broccoli & Egg Salad   27
Broccoli & Mushroom Egg Cups   25
Broccoli-gruyère Soup   21
Buckwheat Pancake With Yogurt & Berries   18

C

Cajun Red Beans   69
Cali Dogs   62
California Frittata Bake   14
Caribbean Turkey Wings   33
Carrot Coconut Cake   75
Celery & Red Bean Stew   61
Cheesy Mushrooms With Garganelli   68
Cheesy Polenta With Sundried Tomatoes   71
Cheesy Shrimp Scampi   54
Cheesy Tuna   53
Chicken & Zucchini Pilaf   30

Chicken Gumbo   32
Chicken Sandwiches With Barbecue Sauce   18
Chili Squid   51
Chimichurri Chicken   36
Chipotle Shredded Beef   46
Chocolate Custard   80
Chocolate Glazed Cake   77
Chorizo Soup With Roasted Tomatoes   21
Chowder With Broccoli, Carrot & Tofu   26
Cilantro Pork With Avocado   43
Cinnamon Applesauce   75
Cinnamon Brown Rice Pudding   81
Cinnamon Roll Doughnut Holes   14
Classic Beef Stroganoff   39
Classic Palak Paneer Dip   23
Coconut Milk Millet Pudding   62
Coconut Millet Porridge   61
Coconut Rice Breakfast   71
Cottage Cheesecake With Strawberries   76
Couscous With Lamb & Vegetables   70
Creamy Chicken Soup   25
Creamy Pesto Chicken   30
Creamy Wild Salmon   51
Creole Shrimp With Okra   55
Crustless Crab Quiche   12
Crustless Power Quiche   15
Curly Kale Soup   58
Curried Chicken With Mushrooms   32

D

Date & Apple Risotto   69
Delicious Pork In Button Mushroom Gravy   40
Dilled Salmon Fillets   48
Dilled Salmon Soup   23
Down South Savory Porridge   68

E

Easy Brown Rice With Sunflower Seeds   72
Easy Cheesy Mac   62
Easy Chicken With Capers & Tomatoes   34
Easy Lamb & Spinach Soup   45
Easy Lemon Cake   78
Easy Pork Fillets With Peachy Sauce   42
Easy Red Lentil Dhal With Spinach   70
Easy Tahini Sweet Potato Mash   58
Easy Wax Beans With Ground Beef   39
Egg Muffins To Go   14

F

French Cheese & Spinach Quiche   17
Frittata With Vegetables & Cheese   22

G

Garbanzo Stew With Onions & Tomatoes   22
Garlic Chicken   34
Georgia Peach French Toast Casserole   16
Gingered Sweet Potatoes   23
Gingery Butternut Squash Soup   62
Grandma's Fruit Compote   79
Greek Yogurt With Honey & Walnuts   18
Greek-style Navy Beans   72
Green Goddess Mac 'n' Cheese   66
Gruyere Mushroom & Mortadella Cups   44

H

Haddock With Edamame Soybeans   52
Ham & Peas With Goat Cheese   67
Hard-"boiled" Eggs   12
Herby Crab Legs With Lemon   50
Herby Trout With Farro & Green Beans   52
Homemade Gazpacho Soup   61
Homemade Spanish-style Horchata   82
Honey Butternut Squash Cake Oatmeal   13
Honey-glazed Turkey   35
Hot Chicken With Coriander & Ginger   31
Hot Chicken With Garlic & Mushrooms   31
Hot Cocoa Brownies   76
Hot Paprika & Oregano Lamb   45
Hot Tofu Meatballs   60

J

Jamaican Chicken With Pineapple Sauce   32
Jamaican Cornmeal Porridge   70

K

Kimchi Ramen Noodle Soup   23
Korean-style Chicken   31

L

Lamb Chorba   40
Lazy Steel Cut Oats With Coconut   19
Leftover Beef Sandwiches   42
Lemon-apricot Compote   79
Lemony Pancake Bites With Blueberry Syrup   19
Lentil Pâté   27
Lentil-spinach Curry   68
Light & Fruity Yogurt   17
Loaded Broccoli   26
Lobster Risotto   49
Louisiana Grouper   54

M

Macaroni With Chicken & Pesto Sauce   34
Maple Pork Carnitas   43
Mediterranean Cod With Capers   55
Mediterranean Cod With Cherry Tomatoes   49
Melt-in-your-mouth Meatballs   41
Mexican Pinto Beans   73
Milk-boiled Corn On The Cob   25
Millet Eggplant Pilaf   57
Mint Salmon On Spinach Bed   53
Molten Chocolate Cake   83
Moroccan Lentil Soup   26
Mushroom-potato Hash Casserole   22

O

Octopus & Shrimp With Collard Greens   50
Orange New York Cheesecake   81

P

Pancetta With Garbanzo Beans   70
Paprika Salmon With Dill Sauce   51
Parmesan Topped Vegetable Mash   59
Pea & Garbanzo Bean Soup   24
Pear & Cider Pork Tenderloin   43
Pie Cups With Fruit Filling   77
Pistachio-crusted Halibut   51
Pizza-style Stuffed Mushrooms   28
Plum & Almond Dessert   82
Pomegranate Rice With Vegetables   71
Pork Chops With Creamy Gravy & Broccoli   39
Pork With Onions & Cream Sauce   44
Potatoes & Tuna Salad With Pickles   25
Power Green Soup With Lasagna Noodles   58
Pulled Pork   42

Pumpkin Muffins   16
Pumpkin Steel Cut Oats With Cinnamon   15

Q

Quick And Easy Meatloaf   44
Quick Cassoulet   57
Quick Chicken Soup   27
Quick French-style Lamb With Sesame   43
Quinoa Bowls With Broccoli & Pesto   67
Quinoa Pilaf With Chicken   34

R

Red Beans And Chorizo   69
Rice Pudding   80
Rigatoni With Turkey & Tomato Sauce   32
Risotto With Broccoli & Grana Padano   72
Root Beer Float Cupcakes   78
Rosemary Potato Fries   26
Rustic Soup With Turkey Balls & Carrots   28

S

Saucy Chicken Marsala   31
Sautéed Spinach With Roquefort Cheese   57
Savory Butternut Squash Soup   22
Savory Spinach With Mashed Potatoes   63
Seafood Chowder With Oyster Crackers   48
Seafood Medley With Rosemary Rice   50
Short Ribs With Wine Mushroom Sauce   40
Shrimp Boil With Chorizo Sausages   52
Shrimp Fajitas   53
Simple Apple Cinnamon Dessert   78
Simple Carrot & Oregano Soup   27
Simple Onion Cheese Soup   24
Smoked Salmon & Egg Muffins   19
Speedy Mac & Goat Cheese   60
Spiced & Warming Mulled Wine   80
Spiced Peaches With Cinnamon Whipped Cream   79
Spicy Haddock With Beer & Potatoes   50
Spicy Honey Chicken   36
Spicy Salmon With Oregano & Sea Salt   55
Spicy Split Pea Stew   58
Spicy Three-bean Vegetable Chili   67
Spinach & Feta Pie With Cherry Tomatoes   17
Spinach-feta Risotto   72
Spring Onion Buffalo Wings   30
Steamed Artichokes & Green Beans   64
Steamed Artichokes With Lime Aioli   60
Steamed Bread Pudding   81

Sticky Chicken Wings   36
Strawberry Jam   18
Stuffed Apples   75
Stuffed Potatoes With Feta & Rosemary   61
Stuffed Tench With Herbs & Lemon   48
Sunday Brunch Sausage Gravy   15
Sweet & Citrusy Chicken Breasts   35
Sweet Polenta With Pistachios   60
Sweet Potato Morning Hash   13

T

Tangy Shrimp Curry   49
Tasty Beef Cutlets With Vegetables   44
Tofu Hash Brown Breakfast   17
Tomato & Feta Pearl Barley   73
Tomato & Mushroom Rotini   71
Traditional Lamb With Vegetables   41
Turkey & Black Bean Chili   33
Turkey Cakes With Ginger Gravy   35
Turkey Stew With Salsa Verde   37
Turmeric Stew With Green Peas   63

V

Vanilla Cheesecake With Cranberry Filling   79
Vegetable Paella   67
Vegetarian Green Dip   63

W

Walnut & Pumpkin Tart   82
Weekend Turkey With Vegetables   33
Western Omelet Casserole   13
Wheat Berry Salad   64
White Bean Cassoulet   59
White Wine Marinated Squid Rings   54
Wild Mushroom Soup   24
Wild Rice Pilaf   66
Wine Pork Butt With Fennel & Mushrooms   45

Y

Yogurt Cheesecake With Cranberries   83

Z

Zucchini Pomodoro   59

Made in the USA
Monee, IL
10 September 2023

42488753R00050